"Without realizing it, many American families have welcomed an unruly guest into their homes: not a long-lost uncle—your TV. In *TV: The Great Escape*, my good friend Bob DeMoss helps us make the break from the machine that tends to take over our lives. And he doesn't just make a persuasive argument for going without TV for a month; he takes you on a delightful literary romp through the lives and stories of those who accepted that challenge. I recommend you read this book and do likewise."

—*Chuck Colson, Author & Culture Critic*

"All parents worry about pop culture's influence on their kids. Bob DeMoss offers a revolutionary, empowering, commonsense approach to bringing that influence under control. His book is well written, uplifting, and entertaining."

—*Michael Medved, Film Critic & Nationally Syndicated Radio Host*

"It is with a great deal of conviction that I wholeheartedly endorse *TV: The Great Escape*. At last a book for people who care about the influence of TV on themselves and on their children. For those of us who wish to control TV rather than be controlled by it, this is must reading."

—*Dr. Tony Evans, Senior Pastor, Oak Cliff Bible Fellowship, Dallas, TX*

" . . . a message for all Americans."

—*George Voinovich, United States Senator, Ohio*

"As a society, I don't think we understand the influential platform we have given television. For some time now my family has been concerned about the largely negative content on TV, and because of this we have experienced firsthand the wonders of an unplugged television! Bravo to Bob for writing this much-needed book."

—*Rebecca St. James, Christian Music Artist & Author*

TV

The Great Escape!

Life-changing Stories from Those
Who Dared to Take Control

Robert G. DeMoss, Jr.

CROSSWAY BOOKS • WHEATON, ILLINOIS
A DIVISION OF GOOD NEWS PUBLISHERS

TV: The Great Escape!

Copyright © 2001 by Robert G. DeMoss, Jr.

Published by Crossway Books
              A division of Good News Publishers
              1300 Crescent Street
              Wheaton, Illinois 60187

Cover design: Cindy Kiple

Cover illustration: Meredith Johnson

First printing, 2001

Printed in the United States of America

Unless otherwise designated, Scripture is taken from the *Holy Bible: New International Version*®. Copyright © 1973, 1978, 1984 by International Bible Society. Used by permission of Zondervan Publishing House. All rights reserved.

The "NIV" and "New International Version" trademarks are registered in the United States Patent and Trademark Office by International Bible Society. Use of either trademark requires the permission of International Bible Society.

Scripture quotations marked NASB are taken from the *New American Standard Bible*® Copyright © The Lockman Foundation 1960, 1962, 1963, 1968, 1971, 1972, 1973, 1975, 1977, 1995. Used by permission. (www.Lockman.org)

Scripture references marked NKJV are taken from the *New King James Version.* Copyright © 1982, Thomas Nelson, Inc. Used by permission.

Library of Congress Cataloging-in-Publication Data
DeMoss, Robert G.
  TV: the great escape! Robert G. DeMoss, Jr.
    p. cm.
  Includes bibliographical references.
  ISBN 1-58134-242-X (trade pbk. : alk. paper)
  1. Television broadcasting—Social aspects. 2. Television broadcasting—
Religious aspects—Christianity. I. Robert G. DeMoss, Jr. II. Title.
PN1992.6.D465   2001
302.23'45—dc21   00-011181
                                                CIP

15	14	13	12	11	10	09	08	07	06	05	04	03	02	01
15	14	13	12	11	10	9	8	7	6	5	4	3	2	1

For my girls,
Carissa and Sienna DeMoss
May your lives be filled with
love, laughter, and the Lord.

CONTENTS

ACKNOWLEDGMENTS

Allow me to thank all of the brave souls who have already participated in the TV-turnoff challenge. Some were motivated by the idea of seeing their name in this book. Others were compelled to take this radical step because they decided TV had robbed them of a life for far too long. The time spent staring at TV starved their relationships of vitality. They were running on empty and ready for anything that might help.

Whatever the motivation, each one—including those who began but didn't go the distance to finish their fast—are champions in my book. Why? They had the guts to do something that many will never try in their lifetime. I say, "Hats off!"

When I described my concern about current trends in pop culture and the need for greater discernment with Marvin Padgett, vice president of editorial at Crossway Books, he immediately resonated with my world-life view. Thank you for believing in this book, Marvin.

I was encouraged when Mark Daniels at WFIL and my brother "Timmy D" at WZZD (stations in Philadelphia) decided to challenge their listenership to take the TV-free challenge. All of us were shocked as more than a hundred listeners called offering to participate. Thank you for using your airwaves to spark such an enthusiastic response.

A word of appreciation goes to Kirby Anderson, host of "Open Line," heard nationwide over the Moody Broadcast Network, who provided me the opportunity to challenge their listeners to go TV-free. Now that the book is done, let's do it again!

I'm also indebted to my father who faithfully pored over the initial draft of these pages and offered his extremely valuable insights. Thanks, Dad, for that labor of love!

My wife, Leticia, did a fantastic job "holding down the fort" while I went into my cave to write for endless hours at a time. And her editorial feedback propelled me across the finish line. Thank you, sweetheart, for sustaining me with your love and sacrifice. And I especially thank my daughter Carissa for her constant prayer support throughout the writing process.

FOREWORD

Let me ask you a question. What percentage of children in America would you estimate have a TV in their bedroom? Ten percent? Twenty-five percent? Are you sitting down? In this eye-opening book, Bob DeMoss cites a Kaiser Family Foundation study reporting that more than fifty percent of children ages two to eighteen years old currently have a TV set by their bedside. Look at it another way: One out of every two children can fall asleep to the drone of a TV set.

I'm forced to wonder, where are the parents?

As I read that alarming statistic, the words of 1 Corinthians 6:12 came to mind: "'Everything is permissible for me'—but not everything is beneficial. 'Everything is permissible for me'—but I will not be mastered by anything."

In other words, nowhere in the Bible will you find "Thou shalt not place a TV in a child's bedroom." At the same time, given the problematic content of much of today's television programming, I'm puzzled why any parents—especially in a Christian household—would willingly invite and permit such a potentially evil influence into the intimate quarters of their impressionable youngsters.

Just look at a typical day in TV land: Sexual themes saturate prime time. Crude language is commonplace. Acts of violence are played for laughs. Parents are portrayed as bumbling idiots. There are far more homosexual characters than people of faith. And the predominant worldview is that of secular humanism. Why, then, does the vast churchgoing body of believers remain hooked on the box? Whatever happened to "do not be conformed to this world, but be transformed by the renewing of your mind" as the apostle Paul urges us in Romans 12:2?

You see, I firmly believe that there is a battle for the heart, mind, and soul of this nation. It is a war between competing worldviews: Christianity and secular humanism. In my view, television is the primary battleground where the humanistic belief system is celebrated. Yet, sad to say, for the most part there is no appreciable difference between the TV consumption in the Christian home and that of their unchurched counterpart.

The net result is that believers find themselves compromising their biblical values. Over time they are left drained of the trans-forming spiritual vitality that is rightfully theirs in Christ. That is why I appreciate the challenge Bob presents in this dynamic, informative, and, yes, entertaining book. As you'll find, Bob's ultimate goal is to point us to the balanced use of television—a place where discernment and the mind of Christ guard our hearts when we sit down to watch.

Television is the most powerful assault on the human mind ever invented, because it combines both the eye gate and the ear gate into the mind. Consequently whoever controls the TV and what it com-municates determines whether TV is good or bad for our children. Unfortunately, many of those who control this powerful medium do not share our Christian moral values. Too much of the wrong kind of TV watching is the main reason we are losing 50 to 70 per-cent of our church kids to the world by the time they graduate from high school.

In this book Bob is helping us get up and out of our recliners long enough to engage in the rich, rewarding real-life experiences that await us once we get reacquainted with our family and God's vast cre-ation. As more Christian families rise to the challenge found in this book, I'm convinced that we as a church can truly be salt and light to a culture that so desperately needs us.

Read on, dear friend, and get ready for the adventure of your lifetime!

Tim LaHaye

INTRODUCTION

Have you ever had one of those nights when you spent the evening surfing across every television channel—at least three times—only to discover "there's nothing on"? Then, rather than turn it off, you decided to watch an infomercial for some "revolutionary new space-age product" or "a diet plan that represents an amazing breakthrough in weight loss."

I've had a number of nights like that, usually when I'm in a hotel on the road. An infomercial for financial freedom comes to mind. You've probably seen it, too. A well-tanned, neatly manicured man sits comfortably at his poolside. Sitting with him are any number of people who represent "true success" stories for following his "proven plan" to wealth and financial security. Oh, and in the background an array of late-model luxury cars are parked in his driveway.

For just three easy payments of $69 each (plus shipping and handling), his astonishing secrets for amassing phenomenal wealth in my spare time will be rushed to me. And if I call before the infomercial ends, he'll toss in a bonus videotape of him brushing his dog Fife as he reveals ten tax breaks so that I'll never need to pay the IRS a penny of these newfound profits.

With bleary, bloodshot eyes (it's now almost 1 A.M.), I fumbled for a pencil to jot down that life-changing toll-free number.

But a tinge of doubt lingered. I never called.

Sometime during the following week, I read an article saying that this same guru was under investigation for fraud.

As the saying goes, "If it sounds too good to be true, it probably is."

No wonder you and I have become distrustful of bold promises. We've been so jaded by bogus claims and fraudulent guarantees that when a legitimate offer comes along, we're naturally suspicious. It's a classic case of guilt by association.

This puts me in an awkward position, because what I'm about to say might just sound "too good to be true." So I'm asking you to hear me out. Let me assure you I'm *not* writing by my pool, and I don't have a dog or luxury car. And there's no toll-free number to call in the next thirty minutes "to avoid bitter disappointment."

Plainly put, I know of a way for you to transform all aspects of your life and, if married, that of your entire family. From increasing the intimacy with your spouse, getting housework and home projects completed, saving extra money, even losing weight, to watching your children develop a love for books, play, and creative expression—they're all within your reach.

Sound interesting?

Best of all, it costs nothing to get started, and the entire process takes just thirty days—although many benefits will be noticed almost immediately. Plus, this book you're holding is the only thing you need to get started.

What's my secret formula for success?

This may surprise you. It's the simple act of sending your TV on a vacation for a month. That's all there is to it.

Here's why. As I've traveled North America over the past twenty years, I found an overwhelming majority of families frustrated with the role of TV in their homes. They confessed to spending far too much time gazing into its colorful glare. They were dismayed at the way their values were often ridiculed. Yet in spite of the declining standards of television content, many said they were "addicted" and could do nothing about controlling the tube.

That's why from the fall of 1999 to the spring of 2000 I challenged families across America to consider clicking off their televisions for thirty days. Afterward they could go back to the use of TV. But for that handful of days, they were permitted to watch no TV at home, no TV at a friend's home, and no TV with their neighbors.

No television anywhere.

No exceptions. None.

Why? It's been my belief that the modest step of turning off the television for a month can and will have a profoundly positive effect on each member of any family who goes TV-free. And, as you'll discover in the pages ahead, hundreds of families have tried going TV-free for thirty days. Those who made it were astonished at the life-changing difference that month made.

I asked them to journal their experience—whether good, bad, or ugly. They did. And now you have the opportunity to eavesdrop on these courageous families who took my challenge. (In the interest of privacy, I use the participants' actual first names only, along with their city and state.) These folks are not superhuman. They, like you, thought that their lives had been dominated by the television for far too long. They knew something drastic had to happen if they were to ever break free from the trancelike hold TV had over them.

Each took the radical step of boxing up their remote controls and unwrapping their self-control. They said good night to Leno one last time before embarking on the trip of their lives.

How about you?

Are there times when you feel that your family life has been in a deep freeze? Have your kids skated off in different directions? Do you watch TV during meals instead of talking with each other? Is your daily routine driven by the TV guide? Does it seem that the intimacy in your marriage has slipped away? Are you always behind in your housework? Do you regret not completing college because of a lack of time?

If the shoe fits, I've got great news: You can get back into the game of life *and win!* There's still time to revive the romance in your marriage or to finish that education you left behind. There's plenty of opportunity to explore a new hobby—or complete an old project long ago abandoned. You can enjoy the most satisfying years of child-raising and even get your housework done with time to spare. Yes, your family life *can* be alive with conversation and brimming with home-grown activities—a nest of creativity. You *can* fall in love with life once again. Most important, you will discover a fascinating part of living that you never knew existed.

"The simple decision to unplug TV for just one month has the power to revolutionize our relationships with our spouse, our children, our world, and most importantly with our God."

But there's a step you'll need to take.

Find a quiet spot. Pour a cup of Java, and let's talk.

If you think this whole idea of going TV-free for a month sounds daunting, I completely understand. After all, to consider the idea of not being entertained by television for a month might come close to thinking about scaling the side of Mount Rushmore. First, you must face the chilly reception of your family, who may think you've missed your annual visit to the doctor.

Then there are the frosty looks from friends and neighbors who think your idea is, well, just a tad crazy. Even though I'm not advocating the elimination of television from your home forever (you'll likely return to a more balanced level of TV use after the month), the thought of going without television for any length of time baffles many.

I can tell you from the experience of those who took the TV challenge that there are both immediate and lasting benefits awaiting the brave soul who dares to go where most fear to tread. Those who have completed their TV-free month have told me that they get more rest, have a more vibrant prayer life—and, yes, have even lost weight!

Take, for instance, Jennifer from Pottstown, Pennsylvania. She actually lost four pounds—but that's nothing compared to what her family gained from taking my challenge (her entire daily journal is featured in a later chapter).

Then there are Ron and Michelle of Dallas, Texas. When I asked if they'd recommend the TV fast to others, without hesitation they responded: "*NEVER!* Unless, of course, they want to develop a deeper relationship with God, their spouse, their children, and friends. And," they added, "only if they want to actively experience life instead of getting fat sitting mindlessly in front of a box."

Listen to Rick from Medina, Ohio, who, having completed the challenge, looked back and confessed, "Actually, after my TV-free month, I feel closer to my wife and children than I have felt perhaps ever."

Throughout these pages you'll be treated to the heartwarming, encouraging words of those pilgrims who've gone before you. At the same time, this is not a pie-in-the-sky book. It includes the trials, temptations, and failures that surface when confronting such a controversial topic. For example, a number of families who initially agreed to unplug their TV changed their minds *before* beginning.

One upset man offered this apology: "Bob, I'm sorry, but my family and I will not be turning off the TV set after all. I've reached a snag—my wife. She seems to think that the television is not on that much and that it's hurting nothing. I still will work on having them shut down. One TV broke the other day, which leaves us with only one more. The Lord willing, that one may also break."

Realistic and honest—that's the stuff you'll find in these pages. What's more, this is not a guilt-trip book. Rather, my desire is to reintroduce you to the riches that real life has to offer. You see, my premise is that the simple decision to unplug TV for just one month has the power to revolutionize your relationship with your spouse, your children, your world, and most importantly with your God.

Incidentally, I recognize that there are three different kinds of readers. One group is highly motivated to get started. They wish they'd had this book years ago. Another kind is hesitant and yet open to the concept. A friendly nudge might just get them to take the first step.

The last kind of reader is totally closed to a TV-free experiment of any length. They cannot see why anyone in their right mind would willingly forgo this national pastime. Perhaps the only reason they've agreed to read this book is that they've been paid to—or threatened. So in between the commercials, this dear soul has reluctantly cracked open the pages . . . just because.

Wherever you find yourself in that mix, let's climb this mountain together. Hang in there. Before long you and your family will be falling in love with life again!

PART ONE

Hollywood Squares

1

Before There Was TV

I find television very educational.
Every time someone switches it on I go into
another room and read a good book.

GROUCHO MARX [1]

In January 1980, a twin-propeller plane pierced the clouds above Arctic Village, Alaska, and landed in the fresh mantle of snow that blanketed the perpetually frozen earth. A lone figure bounded out, opened the rear cargo compartment, and retrieved a strange but unique gift—a twelve-inch black-and-white TV set. The rumor that this amazing box refused to stop talking spread quickly through the Indian tribe.

Gideon James, the happy new owner, carefully carried the TV to his log cabin and, with a host of fellow tribesmen who had crowded into his tiny home, watched channel 9 until two in the morning. That's when the only station they could receive 150 miles above the Arctic Circle finally signed off.

True, few understood the jokes told by the gray-headed, snickering white man named Johnny Carson whose image first filled the tiny screen. But like the pull of a magnet, the talking box drew them irresistibly. These brave Indian tribesmen were powerless to tear themselves away from the surreal spectacle. It was as if the TV had cast a hypnotic spell over the willing subjects who had focused on the grainy picture flickering before them.

Todd Lewan, a reporter from the Associated Press, chronicled the impact of TV on this tiny community of ninety-six people. He spoke with a twenty-five-year-old Indian who recalled that "I wanted to watch it and watch it and watch it. I woke up at 6 A.M. to watch it more. I did this for two weeks. When I went out in the country to hunt, all I could hear was the TV in my head."[2]

Today, Lewan reported, all sixty-seven of the cabins in Arctic Village have at least one TV set. And with the introduction of television, he discovered that the mothers, who for centuries had made ice cream from caribou bone powder and river slush, now craved Ben & Jerry's. They gave up making "tundra tea" from alpine spruce needles, insisting on Folger's instant coffee.

Moccasins were traded in for Nikes.

Wood stoves got zapped by microwave ovens.

Legendary tales around the campfire were exchanged for the latest Seinfeld or Simpson episode.

Little did this ancient Indian tribe know that their way of life would be changed forever—for the worse.

Looking back, Gideon James, a member of the Tribal Council, observed, "The TV teaches greed. It shows our people a world that is not ours. It makes us wish we were something else."[3]

Fellow tribesman James John, at thirty-seven, sounded bitter as he remembered a more vibrant community life prior to the arrival of the unstoppable talking box. "Before the TV, we were a tough people," he lamented. "Not anymore. Now people only go hunting if they have a four-wheeler." And the kids? "All they do now is play board games, watch TV, act like they've done it all."[4]

Twenty years ago the arrival of television was highly anticipated as a good thing, a positive move in the right direction. It would connect this distant tribe to the rest of the globe, bringing them a step closer to being "civilized." Now the city fathers are left to wonder if the promise of TV was just a bad illusion.

SITTING IN FAT CITY

Television's long arm of influence continued its reach around the globe, from the frozen tundra of Alaska to the Fiji Islands in the South Pacific.

The first TV set landed in Fiji as recently as 1995. Prior to the arrival of television, the Fijians had this curious cultural belief that fat was fabulous.

The bigger the body, the better. Large was in charge.

Though hard to believe, for years those living in Fiji considered it a compliment when greeting a friend to say, "Looks like you've put on some weight! You look great!" I'm serious. And, ever-hungry for the perfectly robust bod, the Fijians had created various herbal potions that stimulated their appetite. Unlike our national obsession with getting "abs of steel," they sought "flabs of steel."

But the arrival of Western culture via television's heavy dosage of *Friends, Seinfeld,* and *Baywatch* prompted girls in this island paradise to rethink their picture of beauty. Thanks largely to the (initially) one available channel, young women in Fiji came to believe that robust was revolting.

"'The TV teaches greed. It shows our people a world that is not ours. It makes us wish we were something else.'"

Anthropologist and psychiatrist Anne Becker, a research director at Harvard's Eating Disorders Center, noted that the number of teens at risk for a variety of eating disorders (including anorexia and bulimia) *more than doubled* in Fiji in the three years since their introduction to TV. What's more, she discovered that the use of vomiting as a weight-control technique by high school girls *increased fivefold* during the same period.

A mere coincidence?

In her report Becker observed, "The acute and constant bombardment of certain images in the media are apparently quite influential in how teens experience their bodies. There's a huge disparity between what they see on television and what they look like themselves—that goes not only for clothing, hairstyles and skin color but size of bodies."

Stories such as these cause me to wonder what, if any, the impact of TV-viewing is on the church. When we believers are drawn like moths to television's guiding light, it's only prudent to ask: How might our faith and our values be shaped by what we see?

To that end I asked hundreds of folks from my church several questions in an informal TV survey. For a starter I asked, "How has television had a *positive* effect on your Christian growth?" I thought it was telling that many left the question unanswered. Some cited *Touched by an Angel* and *7th Heaven* as examples of programming that had had a positive impact on their lives. A few pointed to the occasional special on the History or Discovery channel. But the overwhelming majority didn't perceive TV as a positive influence in their home.

How about you?

How has TV had a *positive* effect on your Christian growth?

The second question was: "How has television had a *negative* effect on your Christian growth?" This time the respondents had much to say. Here's a sample:

Anette said, "TV has had a gradually corrosive effect on what's acceptable to me. My standard for holiness can easily become the world's standard instead of God's standard."

Allison said, "It desensitizes me and my family to violence, sex, and worldliness."

Dwayna observed, "It robs me of precious moments I could have spent with God."

Jordon said, "Television celebrates relativism and in a subtle way undermines God's absolute standards for my life."

Gerry said, "I have often found myself numbly staring at it for hours. It dulls my mind and distracts me from important relationships and responsibilities."

The majority confessed that TV usage in the home promoted laziness and was a huge "time-waster."

Again let me put the question to you: "How has TV had a *negative* effect on your Christian growth?"

LIGHTEN UP, BOB!

A handful of people took issue with the notion that there's anything wrong with the content of today's programming or its impact on them. They said I should "lighten up" because it's "only entertainment" and something they do to "unwind and relax."

No biggie.

A way to "de-stress" from a hectic day.

Author John Marks Templeton disagrees with that notion. He notes: "Along with providing short-term relief from stress, television entertainment actually creates changes in the viewer that can prevent him from expressing his greatness."[5] Templeton adds, "Individuals who watch television regularly become passive witnesses of what is projected onto the screen. As a result, they tend to become reactive rather than proactive in their approach to life."[6]

In other words, over time the viewer wallows in passivity.

Real life requires too much effort.

Creativity is left unexplored.

Meaningful conversations are left unspoken.

Relationships remain shallow.

What's more, Templeton says, "Through extended periods of viewing, people tend to grow less discerning; they simply accept what they are shown without regard for the value of its message or aesthetic quality."[7]

Need proof?

Four brief examples from TV land underline this concern.

There's a popular television show sweeping the nation. In it people punch each other with the barbaric zeal of Attila the Hun, pull out their opponent's hair like a ravenous caveman protecting his turf, and spew enough coarse expletives to keep pace with a veteran sailor.

Another night of pro wrestling? Good guess—but no.

Just business as usual on the *Jerry Springer Show*.

And millions of Americans are tuning in—upwards of eight million every day. What's the attraction? Kinky sex—a thirty-two-year-old divorced woman announcing her engagement to her nineteen-year-old stepson. Maybe it's a guest revealing his/her sex change to his/her spouse prior to their marriage. Transvestites. Hookers. Strippers.

Nothing is sacred.

Decadent themes such as these, which would never have been permitted twenty years ago, have propelled the *Jerry Springer Show* audience share to increase by nearly 200 percent in the last year. Springer, in a moment of rare self-disclosure, told an associate, "I know I'm going to hell for this."[8]

If our tastes are like the *Titanic*, then Springer's show is the tip of the scandalous iceberg destined to sink our sensibilities to a new low. Take, for instance, the deal CBS penned with Howard Stern in 1998. Even before the ink was dry, Stern went public to paint a picture of what viewers can expect from his warped imagination. In a press conference he explained, "We'll have sex and nudity and lesbians. Standards have gone down to an all-time low, and I'm here to represent it. It's a miracle; I prayed to God for this."[9]

Although not known for his promotion of traditional family values, Woody Allen got it right when he observed, "In Beverly Hills they don't throw their garbage away. They make it into television shows."[10]

Comedy Central's *South Park* could be considered that kind of trash. Here four animated cartoon tykes wallow in toilet humor and debasing themes. A recent episode entitled "Cartman Gets an Anal Probe" might even make MTV's Beavis and Butthead blush. Flaming flatulence and mutilated animals are all played for laughs in *South Park*. The show is routinely given television's strictest rating of TV-14.

"If our tastes are like the Titanic, then Springer's show is the tip of the scandalous iceberg destined to sink our sensibilities to a new low."

If cartoons aren't your bag, the WB network hopes you'll join the action on *Dawson's Creek*—their highest rated show. Each week there's a one-in-three chance that your teenage daughter will be watching. What will she see? Past story lines have included teacher-student sex, adultery, and impotence. Themes such as these prompt the frequent TV-14 rating.

The evidence suggests that our current cultural climate is unencumbered by a moral compass. As a nation we've traded in reason for a rating system. Common sense for corporate irresponsibility.

Our morally numb society prefers to engage their recliner rather than their brains. This lack of discretion on our part ultimately fuels the networks' race to be racy.

And a generation of young eyes are glued to the screen.

Have I overstated the problem?

Let's take an inventory of the facts.

First, a study of more than 3,000 children in the United States funded by the Kaiser Family Foundation found that 53 percent of all children ages two to eighteen years old now have a television set in their bedroom. Worse, almost half (49 percent) claimed that their parents had provided no rules about what they could and couldn't watch. While many parents have abdicated their God-given responsibility to "train a child in the way he should go," the media elite who have assumed that role have, in their collective wisdom, continued to push the boundaries of decency and acceptability.

"As a nation we've traded in reason for a rating system."

During the final months of 1999, the Parents' Television Council compared the content of television shows during the prime time "family hour" with the same period just two years prior in 1997. They found:

Violence was up 86 percent.

Sexual content was up 77 percent.

Foul language rose 58 percent.

Gary Levin, a columnist for *USA Today*, during the fall of 1999 echoed my concern: "TV was once so pure you couldn't show a roll of toilet paper in a commercial. Today, critics say, TV often resembles a toilet. Never mind protecting the kids from the suggestive banter on *Friends*: Prime time is saturated with sex, and more explicitly so than ever. A look at the TV season that's unfolding this week will leave even jaded viewers stunned at what they see. A scene in Fox's upcoming *Manchester Prep* shows a teen lustily eyeing her stepbrother's manhood in the shower. And the word *penis* is nearly as ubiquitous as the laugh track this fall."[11]

Columnist John Leo puts it this way: "In the old days, the Brady Bunch never thought about sex, as far as we knew. Their modern counterparts on TV never think about anything else."[12] He adds, "These shows are also carriers of heavy cultural messages, the most obvious being that parents are fools. In the teen soap operas, parents are absent, stupid, irrelevant, zanily adulterous, on the lam, or in jail. The unmistakable message is that kids are on their own, with no need to listen to parents, who know little or nothing anyway."[13]

"Our morally numb society prefers to engage their recliner rather than their brains. This lack of discretion on our part ultimately fuels the networks' race to be racy."

And, according to a study commissioned by the Shell Oil Company, 60 percent of Americans believe the decline in moral values is *the most pressing problem facing the nation.* The report surveyed adults to identify what, in their view, were the leading factors contributing to this decline. Families not teaching children good values topped their list (88 percent). The rise in drug abuse was second (83 percent), and the fact that society is too tolerant of bad behavior placed third (80 percent). Fully 73 percent polled said "adult language/sexually explicit TV" contributed to our country's deteriorating morality.[14]

When it's all said and done, the only "winners" are the cash-hungry corporate sponsors and the equally greedy network executives who pollute the public airwaves by putting profits ahead of social responsibility. And yet can we blame them when millions of us, including a vast audience of churchgoing believers, continue to demonstrate an unwillingness to demand better?

AS THE WORLD TURNS

Everywhere television has been introduced, change happens. Some of those changes have been important, even valuable. But more often than not, the changes are undesirable. Why? In TV land it's the value system of a *few* that is inflicted on *the many*. In turn, *the many* make changes in their lives based upon the view from the *few*.

As the picture of life presented by the *few* becomes increasingly tarnished, the changes that take place in the rest of us—if we're honest—are alarming. We've come to tolerate the intolerable. It's been said, television brings people into our living rooms whom we wouldn't permit to come through the front door.

What's worse, we've wasted our precious time feeding on electronic Twinkies. Above and beyond all this, the real tragedy is something else: Our excessive TV indulgence robs us of precious time that can never be replaced. A conversation with a child struggling with homework, a helpful phone call to someone in need, reading a book that might elevate our spirits and stimulate our imagination—these opportunities are lost forever.

"Sixty percent of Americans believe the decline in moral values is the most pressing problem facing the nation."

If, as I and other conservative media pundits maintain, television's influence on society is largely negative, what's a poor couch potato to do? Some have proposed participation in a letter-writing campaign to network executives. Others prefer boycotting advertisers. And, of late, there are those who favor the longer-term strategy of "infiltrating" Hollywood with writers, actors, and producers who possess a Judeo-Christian perspective.

While each of these approaches has merit, there's another option. I believe this alternative can produce the fastest results for your family. It's simply to send your TV on an extended vacation. Give it a rest for, say, thirty days and watch what happens!

I believe that the simple decision to unplug TV for a month has the power to revolutionize our relationships with our spouse, our children, our world, and most importantly with our God. How? It's a matter of our focus. In the words of the apostle Paul: "Since, then, you have been raised with Christ, set your hearts on things above, where Christ is seated at the right hand of God. Set your minds on things above, not on earthly things" (Col. 3:1-2).

Take, for instance, Tom and Vicki from Jacksonville, Florida. They were fed up with the state of television and needed to change the focus in their home. They decided out of desperation to give my thirty-day TV-free challenge a try. After just a handful of days they sent me this note: "Bob, our children who *never* get along, much less play together, are getting along and playing together. We even put them in the same bedroom! *It's really weird.* It makes we wonder if the TV had something to do with it since that's the only thing that has changed."

"Television brings people into our living rooms whom we wouldn't permit to come through the front door."

And James and Debbie from Austin, Texas, told me, "The greatest gift to me of having the TV off for a month has been the gift of time. Time for the kids' imaginations to take hold to creatively express themselves."

Later you'll read what many others have eagerly reported.

Are you ready for a radical change? Do you desire to take back the control of your life from TV and begin really living? Would you value a more balanced role for television in your home? Great! In the pages ahead I'll show you and your family how to really fall in love with life in a whole new way.

I assure you the rewards are remarkable for those who try!

2

Try It — You'll Like It

I don't watch television.
I stopped several years ago.

JOHN GRISHAM
BEST-SELLING AUTHOR[15]

In 1997 the Washington Capitals were one of the hottest hockey teams on ice, ultimately skating their way into the Stanley Cup finals. But by the fall of 1999, they had slipped to the brink of disaster with one of the worst records in the NHL. On the road they won a measly five games while losing a dozen and tying another.

Coach Ron Wilson decided that drastic measures were necessary and hastily changed their strategy from an offensive approach to playing more defense. Yet injuries abounded, and the losses mounted. The team was skating on thin ice and couldn't quite figure out what was wrong. Embarrassed by their dismal showing, the team fired their trainer and found a new set of doctors. In spite of the adjustments, they experienced no significant improvement.

Just before Christmas the team embarked on a late-night seven-hour flight from Vancouver and did what they typically do on a flight of that duration: They popped in a video to pass the time. To unwind. To lick their wounds.

That's when the unexpected happened.

The VCR froze.

Sorry, sports fans. No TV tonight.

As the plane winged its way through the evening sky, one by one the players broke the ice and started talking with each other. Out of necessity, they rediscovered the ancient art of conversation. Team goaltender Olaf Kolzig noticed that the "guys got together and talked about how the season was going, what direction it was going in, what we could do better, why we got smoked on the road."[16]

They talked strategy. Obstacles. Key plays. By the time the plane touched down, the Capitals had picked apart their game and knew what needed to be done. After that they were virtually unstoppable—including an eleven-game winning streak.

Later, when asked about the change in the team spirit and performance, Kolzig reflected, "Maybe it was fate the VCRs didn't work. It gave us a chance to just roam about the plane and talk with guys. It was a good way to clear the air." That plus a three-day rest, and, he adds, "we seemed to come back with a renewed sense of pride, and we've played great ever since."[17]

Indeed.

They went 12-2-3 after the broken-VCR incident.

LIFE—WHAT HAPPENS WHILE YOU'RE WATCHING TV

Amazing things happen when you and I pull away from the TV. Just ask the Washington Capitals.

Or consider the hundreds of surveys and journal entries that went into the preparation for this book. When I asked participants for a few benefits of going TV-free for thirty days, at the top of the list was *conversation*. Without a TV, which like a spoiled brat is constantly vying for our attention, we're free to log more talk time with one another.

And when we talk, that personal interaction leads to the intimacy of *knowing and being known* by the people closest to us—our spouse, our kids, other loved ones.

Our Lord.

For instance, Priscilla from Martenez, Georgia, told me that their family decided to put away their TV and, instead of watching the Discovery channel, "we discovered each other."

Or take Ann from Conshohocken, Pennsylvania. She was motivated to take the TV challenge because "for years I've been saying that our TV comes between us, leaving no room for conversation!" By the third TV-free day she made this note in her journal: "My husband and I have had much more time together, and it seems like we don't have a third wheel in our relationship."

David and Theresa from Antioch, Tennessee, who participated in my TV-turnoff challenge made a new habit: "Now we eat around the dinner table together every night. No more vacuuming under TV trays by the couch!" In fact, they enjoyed their TV-free home so much that "a full week went by after our thirty days were up before we even plugged in the TV. My family visited that first week after the TV fast, and we spent the evening talking with no television on. Unheard of!"

Yet millions of Americans, largely out of habit, run to the familiar drone of the television during mealtime, in between meals, after dinner, and well into the night, which effectively stifles all significant dialogue. Why? On the surface TV provides the illusion of community—of being connected to interesting, colorful people.

Yet a look at the way many Americans consume TV in the home (Dad and Mom have a TV in their bedroom, junior is watching in the den, sissy has her own set in her bedroom) reveals that television has had the exact opposite impact on family life. With TV around we live together—all alone.

Call it mutual isolation.

We're collectively separate.

I maintain that even if everything presented on television were wholesome, uplifting, instructive, and pro-social, for the most part the act of watching TV divides people from each other. The longer we stroll the virtual streets of television, the longer we remain detached from the significant others in the real world.

Perhaps the most moving example of this dynamic is from David of Orlando, Florida. Single and in his early thirties, David recalled, "In many ways I feel that I was deprived of parents because of the invention of TV. My folks are in their fifties, and they watch TV every night. EVERY NIGHT. They plan the week by what programs are on. When I was growing up, their attention was *always* on the TV. I could speak to them *only* during the commercials. I can still hear my mom's voice say, 'Not now. The show's started—wait until the commercials.' Other times Dad would bark, 'Can't you see we're trying to watch TV?' To this day, they still sit there staring at the box for hours every night."

How incredibly tragic! Wouldn't you agree?

David recently moved to Japan. When he came home to visit with his parents, he noticed that they maintained their spot ensconced in front of the TV. David commented, "They sat there mesmerized by the television. I felt they saw me as a distraction to their TV routine. I'm amazed how they chose to miss out on real interaction with their son, whom they don't see often, in favor of the television."

"On the surface TV provides the illusion of community—of being connected to interesting, colorful people."

To live in another culture provides a unique perspective. Yet David couldn't help but notice the homogeneity he found both at home and abroad. He sent me this E-mail from overseas: "Bob, it used to be that you could go somewhere else, and people thought differently. But now any state, any town—and in many countries—people all plug into the same mind-control mechanism. I find that people talk about the same things in the same ways. And what a coincidence—it's all in line with the things that folks on TV talk about and in the same way."

As you'll see in chapter five, part of the reason for this universal dialect stems from the way TV provides both the *script* and the *images* to go along with it so that our minds don't have to do any heavy lifting. Unlike other mediums such as radio, books, or music, TV leaves little room for originality, creativity, or individuality of thought.

In the end, while television *divides us from each other*, it *unites us* with "sameness"—with an unimaginative approach to life. A study conducted by pediatrician Dr. Susan Johnson concurs: "Television keeps us sitting, leaves little room for meaningful conversations and seriously impairs our ability to think."[18]

Jerry Mander, author of *Four Arguments for the Elimination of Television*, is deeply concerned about this inability to be discerning while being spoon-fed images. His book explores the semi-comatose state the body enters into during viewing TV. And he describes how this relaxed state of mind puts the viewer at risk to receive ideas he might otherwise reject. At best, Mander asserts, TV effectively transforms viewers into passive consumers.

"Unlike other mediums such as radio, books, or music, TV leaves little room for originality, creativity, or individuality of thought."

While I agree with his concern, there's a greater risk. Television tends to stifle spiritual pursuits and true matters of the heart.

David agrees. He observed, "While entertaining, TV doesn't make anyone happy. It just keeps us from having valuable interaction with family and friends. It stifles individuality and creativity and distracts us from the fullness and beauty of life."

BAND-AIDS VS. SOUL SURGERY

There's an old story about a young man who felt that his life was empty. In a quest for meaning and purpose, he sought the counsel of a wise sage. "My son," the sage started, "seek God, and you will find life's meaning."

The young man appeared puzzled. "How does one find God?" he asked. The sage motioned that he should follow him a short distance down to the river. Not a word was spoken as they waded out to the middle. The cold water flowed just below their chins. Without warning the old sage seized his pilgrim by the shoulders and pushed him under the water. While the startled young man flailed about, the sage continued to hold his head under.

After a prolonged minute, the sage released him. As the young man surfaced, both knew that a moment longer underwater would have meant death. As they headed back to the river bank, the sage remained silent. His student staggered behind him, gasping for oxygen. With effort he managed to ask, "What does that crazy stunt have to do with finding God?"

The thoughtful guru answered with a question of his own. "While you were beneath the surface of the river, what did you long for more than anything else?"

"Air. I had to have air more than anything," came the reply.

The elder man nodded and then explained, "When you desire God as much as you longed for air, you will most certainly find Him."

In a way that illustrates our deeper dilemma.

When it comes to matters of the spirit, we must "be still" and know that the Lord is God. Yet my flesh is unwilling to part with TV long enough for God's Spirit to speak. So on one hand we *say* we want to know God, but on the other hand our preoccupation with television keeps us from hearing from Him. We obviously don't long for God "more than anything."

That's another benefit awaiting those who place their TV on a thirty-day vacation. Without the constant "noise" and chatter of TV filling our world, our mind has the precious space it needs to be truly still before God. In the quiet moments, we can get down to business with God.

For example, Alan, in Decatur, Illinois, who "was very good at turning the set on but lousy at turning it off," found the first few days of his TV-free month manageable. But in the silence that followed, he soon discovered that "TV had been a way for me to drown out and not deal with my inner issues, my unhappiness, and my spirit's needs."

Then there's Leah from Wyoming, Michigan, who is single and who owned two television sets for company. After taking the TV-free challenge, she remarked, "Through all this extra time for thought and personal growth, I discovered I was painfully lonely, I hated my job, and I was largely dissatisfied with myself. I had been using TV the way others will use alcohol or cigarettes, as a way out—something to distract me from the real world. It's raw stimulation but with no purpose. If I don't have to think about these issues much, I don't have to face them."

Without the TV competing for her time, Leah made a point of focusing on God. She said, "God's Word revealed to me so much about myself both that disgusted and inspired me—my self-centeredness, my lack of concern for others, my quickness to anger, my constant complaining and ungrateful heart, my desire to grow in the Spirit, and my lack of discipline to do anything about it." But her story doesn't end there. She said, "Where hours and hours of mindless television trained me in self-indulgence and laziness, I was now training myself in self*less*ness and giving and learning to love others."

"'TV had been a way for me to drown out and not deal with my inner issues, my unhappiness, and my spirit's needs.'"

Another individual who was contemplating the TV turnoff expressed the desire to finally "put into action my prayers that God would change my heart and draw me closer than ever to Him. Although I don't watch too much TV, it does have a hold on my life. Perhaps by cutting out this subtle distraction, I'll be free to truly seek Him above all else!"

Perhaps indeed.

That's what Karen from Glassboro, New Jersey, experienced. She said, "Prayer for some reason has been hard for me in the past because I've been so tired and just have the energy to get to bed. But with the TV off, I'm well rested, and my personal prayer time fits in nicely. It feels good to talk with God."

How about you?

Would you like a more dynamic prayer life?

Do you long to grow closer to God?

Could you use more time talking with members of your family?

When's the last time your imagination had freedom to roam?

How's your hockey game?

Whatever the need, I'm positive that a TV-free month will, like a power washer, blast away the soot and grime that has darkened the window to your spirit for far too long.

How can I be so sure?

Take it from Leah: "In short, my life has been radically transformed because I took a few days out of my life last October to avoid an all-too-easy distraction (TV) and to focus on and develop in myself the things that really matter."

In other words, try it—you'll like it.

No. You'll *love* it!

Everywhere I speak, I challenge the audience to consider going TV-free for thirty days. Here's how Sabrina and her mother living in Fernandina Beach, Florida, responded on one such occasion:

Dear Bob,

My mom and I attended your Learn to Discern seminar over in Callahan, Florida. At the end of the evening when you suggested that families go thirty days without TV, my mom lit up like a Christmas tree. Tomorrow we're gonna start. You see, my two brothers have recently come home to visit and have forgotten to leave. They've taken over the den where our TV lives, so they have taken this news rather badly.

In fact, I just overheard one brother telling my mom, "I can't go without TV! I'm gonna have to find someone to go stay with so I can watch." Maybe this is God's answer to my prayers. Their lifestyle is so different from mine. My mom shows them unconditional love. I, however, want to hit them with a frying pan! I called the cable company myself and told them we want a thirty-day vacation from television. Can't wait to start in the morning!

How about you? Are you ready to rise to the TV-free challenge? Or are you still undecided?

Lisa from San Francisco, California, had misgivings about the duration of the fast. She wrote, "No TV for thirty days, huh? That seems really hard. How about a week at first to kind of warm up?"

Nice try.

Lisa needs to meet Betty from Chester, Pennsylvania. Betty, who is married and has two young boys, took the plunge and announced they'd be turning off the TV. Her kids "decided to play the piano, read books, and talk with each other. They didn't die. They didn't cry. And, as a matter of fact, we all had a great time!"

Like Lisa, Keith and Karen from St. Leonard, Maryland, were stuck in the "undecided zone" when the most remarkable thing happened.

Karen writes, "While my husband and I were trying to decide whether to participate in this turnoff, the TV just wouldn't turn on! Literally. We pushed the button—nothing happened. We're not sure what's wrong with the thing. But it did make our decision a whole lot easier!"

A week after being spontaneously coerced into participation, Keith and Karen wrote in their journal, "No one seems to notice the TV isn't on. I made curtains for the kitchen and covered the kitchen chairs to match. Keith has just about finished our second bathroom, which he started four YEARS ago, and our third grader has read two whole books this week. And our five-year-old and I take the dog for many more walks than we ever did before! Divine intervention??? Sure seems like it. We may never watch TV again!"

Jeff and Suzanne in Caledonia, Mississippi, knew the TV was getting out of control in their home. Suzanne writes, "We have a TV in our room, a TV in son Jake's (age seventeen) room, and a TV in the living room. Since we can't agree on TV shows or movies, we usually rent several videos and watch TV in three different rooms. Terrible, isn't it?"

Once again, an amazing thing "accidentally" happened. Suzanne continues, "Our power went off a couple of weeks ago, and our whole family played Monopoly for about two and a half hours. That's something we hadn't done in about three or four years." They were on their way.

Looking back, she reflected, "We complained about the children 'not helping out' around the house, but TV was the main reason their chores weren't getting done."

As I asked earlier, are you ready to go for it? I certainly hope so. I'm confident you *can* do it, and I'm convinced you will remember these days as a high point in your family's life.

So let's get started!

3

Whose Idea Was This, Anyway?

Television has proved that people
will look at anything rather than each other.

ANN LANDERS [19]

You're a special breed. You've got the courage to be different, to try something most will never attempt in their entire lifetime. You have the guts to find out: "What would life be like without TV?"

What's more, your experiences have the power to energize others who will be watching your bold lead. Some who hear your story will, like you, choose to step out of television's bluish flicker and into the light of real life. They, too, will fall in love with life again.

Here then are the details of your TV-free month. You and your family may select any thirty-day period to take the TV challenge. I'd recommend sooner rather than later, since you've mustered the will to go for it. Whenever you choose to begin, here are a few guidelines to maximize your experience.

OFF LIMITS

As a family, you all agree to watch no television for thirty consecutive days. This means at home, at a friend or relative's house, in a hotel, at the hair dresser, at a laundromat, or at the office (unless directly related to your job).

No TV. Period.

But don't worry. Television *isn't* like food, air, water, sleep—a necessity! You can do this.

No TV includes *no* video rentals or home movies (see exception).
No TV includes not using Nintendo or Sony Playstation.

No TV includes exercise videos. Ouch! Now that's too much of a stretch for Rebekah from Vidalia, Georgia, who sent me a friendly note taking issue with this rule. "I respectfully disagree with no exercise videos. It's for my health! I think I'll need to fudge three times per week on this one."

My view is that walking, jogging, or some other aerobic workout is a better choice than turning to the TV—just for these thirty days. In the absolutely worst-case scenario (a blizzard, a tornado watch, or localized flooding that prevents outdoor activity), I'd allow Rebekah to "listen" to the video workout tape rather than watch it. Just keep a thick cover over the screen and instead picture in your mind what the instructor is doing.

But beware. Television is everywhere.

You'll need to avoid watching while sitting in the doctor's office waiting room. In the mall. At the airport in the boarding area. And, if you live in either Chicago or New York City, be forewarned: You'll encounter a TV in the *elevator* at the Hilton Towers. (Some folks gotta have their TV for the twenty-second ride to their floor.) Just like secondhand smoke, you must attempt to evade "secondhand TV" in these public places.

This might mean making a sacrifice. When Mary from Los Angeles went to do her laundry at a coin-operated facility, she found she had to sit in the smoking section. She told me that was the only spot where there wasn't a television "cackling away in the corner."

"Just like secondhand smoke, you must attempt to evade 'secondhand TV' in these public places."

And picture Janice from Lansdale, Pennsylvania. She "went to visit my brother who has a large-screen TV. Naturally, it was on the whole time we came to be with him. So my son and I spent some time looking at the pictures on the wall in another room. I don't think I would have enjoyed the photos on the wall if I was not trying to avoid television!"

Some brother!

She added, "Oh, have you ever watched other people watching TV? You should try it. . . . Sometimes that's the only way to stick to my TV-free program."

You'll also want to avoid certain known "trouble spots" such as Best Buy, Circuit City, or other mass merchandisers who see fit to light their store with hundreds of flickering TV screens. Likewise, avoid the ESPN Zone, a sports and entertainment facility with some 165 TVs placed everywhere—even in the bathrooms.

WHAT YOU CAN DO

You *can* read as many newspapers and magazines as you like. You may listen to radio. Play board or card games. Enjoy music. Play a computer game—including the responsible use of Gameboy. Get lost in a book. Use the Internet. Savor long walks. Linger at the dinner table for conversation and storytelling. Study your Bible. Engage in sports. Finish a project. Start a puzzle. Introduce yourself to your neighbor. Take a night course. Go swimming. Make a model airplane. Take a drive in the country. Even bungee jump. Fly a kite. Or write the next great novel. Naturally, these choices should reflect wisdom, good taste, and a sense of balance.

There's another thing you can do: You can call the cable company and cancel your service for the month. This signals to the family that you're *committed* to making this work. You're jumping in with both feet—not sticking in a tentative toe to test the water. Don't worry. At the end of your TV-free month, the cable company will still be there—ready, willing, and able to once again "hook" you up and take your money.

THE EXCEPTION

I'm a reasonable person. If necessary, you may watch *one* video a week and *one* movie at the theater a week.

Did I mention that's not one video per person?

Select a video or movie the entire family can view together. Make these rare occasions a special treat. In our home we sometimes have a "dinner theater" where my wife, Leticia, fixes a yummy meal, my daughter Carissa and I either rent a movie or pick one from the family library, and then we all watch it while eating off dinner trays.

For the record, your film choice may *not* be from the television schedule—such as a Sunday evening film classic on PBS, Disney, or the like. Nor can it be from a cable or satellite source for that matter. Most local grocery stores have videos for rental as inexpensively as ninety-nine cents. By renting rather than re-entering the broadcast TV zone, you avoid commercials and minimize the temptation to "just see what's on."

Why do I allow this provision?

Am I getting soft?

Hardly. I'm open to this exception because the ultimate goal is to regain a sense of *balance* with the use of TV. This provision allows you to: 1) plan ahead for the Friday night family film; 2) pick out an appropriate selection; and, 3) discuss afterwards what's been watched, for the TV will be off.

Brad and Beth from Green Bay, Wisconsin, raised a good point of clarification. They noticed that their church routinely used a movie or video clip from *Veggie Tales* or some other Christian-oriented video with the children on Sunday. Their kids wonder if that "counts for their weekly video." I would say it doesn't. However, I'd want to dig deeper and find out why the children's church service is dependent on video tapes rather than "old-fashioned" storytelling.

WHAT IF?

It's possible that you or a member of your family may give in to temptation and watch the tube. What then? Are you disqualified? Should you give up or wallow in a late-night TV binge? No way. Go back to the cold turkey approach and make a note in your journal of what happened and why. Chapter 7 includes a wonderfully honest journal where a participant did happen to give in to temptation—and how she handled it.

Mike from Jacksonville, Florida, raised another sticky question, which you may face, too. He writes:

> *Dear Bob,*
> *I am in a bind. My daughter Kayla and I signed up for the one month without television. But my wife and son refuse to join us. Therefore, we would not be able to do it as a family as you suggest. What should I do?*

Mike's in a tough spot because, as they say, if everyone isn't paddling the boat in the same direction, you'll go nowhere fast. As the spiritual leader in the home, the larger task is to preserve family love and unity, which means Mike may have to be gracious and understanding since Mom and Brother are not on board with the idea.

"The ultimate goal is to regain a sense of balance with the use of TV."

After all, my "TV-free" idea was to increase family closeness—not destroy it. I believe that even in this uncooperative environment, those who desire to try the TV-free experiment can still do so. In Mike's case, he and Kayla must understand that they'll probably bump into Mom or Brother watching the tube. When that occurs, it would be best to keep from making any comment on their choice to watch.

Be loving. Be understanding.

And find something else to do.

Avoid the appearance of being "holier than thou" with little verbal jabs—you know, something along the lines of, "Well, I guess I'll go expand my mind by reading *Hamlet*. It's nothing like Plato's *Republic*, which I finished this morning. But then again, most video veggies wouldn't understand."

The goal is to avoid driving a wedge of resentment into the heart of your home. However, if at any point a rift between "us" and "them" becomes noticeable, I'd recommend that you work at loving each other—even if it means postponing your TV fast for now.

Look at it this way. Many homes are a place where at least one person is on a diet. Maybe it's Mom. Perhaps it's Dad or one of the kids. Everyone doesn't have to eat the dieter's food—just the person(s) on the diet. In the same way, though less ideal, you can go on a TV diet even if family members opt out.

DON'T TOUCH THAT DIAL

Allow me to make a couple of suggestions. First, if possible gather your television sets together and place them in a closet, the basement, or garage. At least unplug the set and turn it toward the wall. If you have a giant-sized unit, consider covering it with a blanket. The goal is to *make it difficult* to slip back into the habit.

On this point, with a smirk Rick from Medina, Ohio, asked his wife, Sandy, to "run down to Wal-Mart and pick up the official Bob DeMoss TV Turnoff Challenge TV Cover with its affordable $19.95 suggested retail price!" In their journal they added, "How's that's for an idea, Bob, huh?"

Actually, it's got potential!

Secondly, why not bring out the games, arts 'n' crafts, puzzles, and books where they can be easily reached. There's nothing like the power of suggestion to point family members toward alternative activities.

And why not use this time to get more involved with the Scriptures? Since you won't be rushing through dinner in order to catch a show, you have time to linger over a family devotion. This doesn't have to be a Bible study on a par with seminary-level studies. Just consider looking up passages on renewing the mind and putting on the mind of Christ.

I'd also like to underline something important: I don't believe that watching television is inherently a sin. I don't consider myself more "holy" if I avoid the tube. At the same time, we found that TV was taking up far too much time in our home. That's why we have chosen to limit its place in the DeMoss household. You can, too!

While you jump into this exciting experiment, you might want to read a book or two on the subject. For example, I've written *Learn to Discern* (Zondervan) and *21 Days to Better Family Entertainment* (Zondervan). Both are available at Christian book stores or from the Internet (iBelieve.com and Amazon.com).

Other key books include *Four Arguments for the Elimination of Television* by Jerry Mander (William Morrow & Company), *Amusing Ourselves to Death* by Neil Postman (Viking), and *Hollywood vs. America* by Michael Medved (HarperCollins).

I am convinced that you are going to be a part of something that could spark revival first in our homes, which will flow into revival in our churches throughout America. And it's worth repeating: Something so simple as minimizing television in our lives has the power to revolutionize our relationships with our spouse, with our children, and most importantly with the Lord.

THE HEART OF THE MATTER

Everyone has his or her own reason(s) for taking the TV-turnoff challenge. Many want more out of life. Some desire more rest. Others describe themselves as "addicted" and just can't seem to get anything done. Or perhaps they don't like the influence television has over their spouse and children.

For Glenda from Phoenix, Arizona, her motivation stemmed from the way TV got in the way of meals and personal devotions. She writes, "Sometimes I'm so involved in what's happening on the TV, it's 8:30 P.M. before I ever make it into the kitchen to start dinner. Or I tell myself that I want to read the Bible but end up watching TV until I'm too tired to read. We have an eight-month-old son, and I refuse to raise him in front of the TV."

How about you?

What reason inspires you to consider going TV-free for a month? Don't rush past this step. When someone asks you, "Whose idea was this, anyway?" you can lay the "blame" on me. I don't mind. However, it's much more meaningful if you could point to something deeper—a longing of your heart, a quest for a richer quality of life, or a goal you've set for the family.

In fact, once you've identified your core motivation, why not jot that down at the beginning of your journal? When you've reached the end of your TV-free month, you'll be able to look back and see how the Lord satisfied that desire.

4

What, No Barney?

*My younger brother thinks we've been brainwashed
and wants your home phone number.*

SUSAN, AN ELEVEN-YEAR-OLD
IN ALBANY, NEW YORK

There will come a point in time when you make "the big announce-ment" to your children. Some families opted for democracy and took a vote before committing to the TV-free month. That's fine, although I believe you as a parent have the right to take the lead, and I prefer that you take charge this time. Either way, the reactions you can expect will range from utter disbelief ("I can't live without TV!") to enthusiasm (as one unusually ambitious fourteen-year-old com-mented, "Dad, forget just one month—let's go for three").

More than likely there will be a mixture of emotions, most bor-dering on despair. This really shouldn't come as a surprise. If a child (or adult) has never gone a day without television and believes life is just peachy the way it is, it's natural for the person to scratch his or her head at your "cuckoo" idea (as one youngster put it).

Don't let such feedback deter your resolve.

At the same time, it's important to encourage your children to express how they feel about this experiment. Ask them what they think will happen once you send your TV on vacation. Start your-selves as parents and take turns describing any fears or misgivings all of you might have. This demonstrates that you're listening and care about their perspective.

For instance, the kids in Kevin and Connie's clan in LeRoy,

Illinois, raised concerns about "some major disaster" that might happen, and they wouldn't be informed about it. That's a common theme I noted in the responses by children. You can assure them that radio and the Internet both provide up-to-the-minute reports on such crises, so there's really nothing to worry about.

When Rick and Sandy's clan from Medina, Ohio, gathered to discuss their pending TV-free month, Mom started off expressing her concerns. Sandy said, "TV is a great resource to keep my toddler 'happy' while I'm trying to prepare dinner. It's much easier to plop him down on a pillow in front of the TV every once in a while when he's especially fussy than to have him literally hanging on my legs as I cook at the stove. Now what will I do with him?" Dad said, "I fear the withdrawal pains. I love watching sports and fear being tempted to watch when I'm elsewhere."

Their eight-year-old wondered, "What if we have a flood warning on TV, and they don't announce it on the radio?" (Again assure children that even the weather channel has full reports on the Internet.) Their six-year-old noted, "We'll be at Grandma's house for three days, and she has cable so we always watch TV there. Now what can I do?" (For starters, why not ask Grandma about some of the activities and games she remembers playing when she was young.)

"You can assure them that radio and the Internet both provide up-to-the-minute reports on such crises, so there's really nothing to worry about."

In the case of Allen from Pontotoc, Mississippi, his daughter worried about "looking stupid in front of my friends who do watch TV. Because I'm not watching TV, I won't get to talk about the same things."

In some cases you might have a young person who cries at the thought of having no TV. He or she appears to be more attached to that electronic box than to, say, a pet, and grieves at its passing. For example, as you'll see in one of the journals I've included in chapter 7, Emily announced that if this was the decision her family wanted to make, she was "officially no longer in our family." She thundered out of the family meeting up to her room propelled by a stormy attitude.

But get this.

After she and her family completed their TV-free month, Emily was the one who enjoyed the time the most! Her brother Brad enjoyed it, too. He said, "I think the TV-free month was very, very fun. TV is kind of boring, so I'm only sort of looking forward to watching it again. It makes me grumpy." After he made his observation, his mother noted, "Brad turned to his sister and said, 'Hey, Emily, let's play,' and they ran off!"

Part of your pre-TV-free announcement should include painting the picture of the fun things you can do together. Expand their horizons. I assure you their initial alarm at being bored in all likelihood will quickly pass.

In the case of Chelsea, she exclaimed on day two of her family's fast that she "couldn't live without TV!" But by day four she was helping her mother with work around the house and discovered new ways to play. Within two weeks, her mother said, "Things are going really great. The kids don't ask to watch TV. They've been spending all their time just playing like kids!"

By the way, my sister Becky Wilson is, in my humble opinion, the most creative kindergarten teacher in all of Philadelphia. She has found the book *Aunt Chip and the Great Triple Creek Dam Affair* by Patricia Polacco to be a wonderful resource with youngsters.

She tells me that the story centers around a decision to give up the habit of reading books in exchange for the habit of watching TV. Polacco illustrates how this change affected the townspeople and prompts young people to think in terms of striking a balance with their media choices. Becky says it's a fantastic discussion starter, one you might want to use as you seek to expand your young people's thinking on the subject.

ALL MY CHILDREN

Should your determination begin to falter in the wake of your children's protests, take comfort from those pilgrims who have gone before you. Remind yourself of the benefits your family will reap in the days and weeks ahead. And, when the objections surface, keep in mind, "this too shall pass."

By day six, for instance, Richie and Julie from Bloomsburg, Pennsylvania, said, "My kids are reading to each other. What more can I say?"

"Things are going really great. The kids don't ask to watch TV. They've been spending all their time just playing like kids!"

Looking back at their TV-free month, David and Theresa from Antioch, Tennessee, noted, "Kellum now has several 'favorite' CDs. I wouldn't say he *prefers* music to TV, but he definitely asks for the music *first*. Pretty good for a two-year-old who fell into the Barney/Teletubbies trap."

Donna from Norman, Oklahoma, admitted, "The first week was the hardest. The kids would get up and immediately ask to turn it on. *NO*. Then in the afternoon they would ask if they could watch a certain program. *NO*. We actually went through withdrawal symptoms of being edgy, grumpy, and fidgety as we purged our minds of the TV. Now my kids get up in the morning and play house, play with their dolls, toys, or whatever suits them. And they love to read books."

Donna's brother wasn't convinced. He couldn't believe she could be "so cruel" to her kids. He said, "I'm going to report you for cruel and unusual punishment." When he asked how they were keeping up with the world, Donna told him, "We are *reading* newspapers."

His response? "Why read it yourself when you can have someone do it for you?"

Some people just don't get it.

In addition to the life-enhancing changes your kids will enjoy, don't forget those benefits you and your spouse will savor. Sue from Lansdale, Pennsylvania, was by her own admission "addicted to sitcoms" and confessed, "Even if I've seen the soaps three or four times already, I'd watch them again." Thanks to the TV-free experience, "laundry got done sooner, the kitchen stayed cleaner, and I look back on those six weeks as the most productive weeks of last year!"

She made one other discovery: "I also look at time differently now. Time didn't come in half-hour chunks, with chores being sandwiched into the commercial breaks and bedtime at the end of a show. If I was out running errands, I didn't have to be home at a certain time to catch my favorite show—it was very freeing."

"'I look back on those six weeks as the most productive weeks of last year!'"

Which brings me to Vicki from Jacksonville, Florida, who learned a number of valuable lessons. For starters, Vicki observed, "I now see that TV is like a drug. It hypnotizes and renders you dependent on it for amusement and entertainment. I remember being a kid and playing outside. When Mom would call me in—as she'd always have to—I'd be so dirty that sometimes she couldn't recognize me. I remember playing elaborate pretend games that would be continued from day to day. If it wasn't raining, you could find all the kids outside. There was never a shortage of playmates."

I love her new motto: "So now I say, 'Go get dirty, kids—we have plenty of soap!'"

What a great perspective.

Maybe I should seek an endorsement from Mr. Bubbles.

5

It's All in Your Mind

TV gives everyone an image,

but radio gives birth to a million images in a million brains.

PEGGY NOONAN

PRESIDENTIAL SPEECH-WRITER [20]

If you've read this far, I imagine you're probably just crazy enough to give the turnoff a try. If so, good for you! I'm confident that the Lord has some wonderful experiences in store for you and your family. At the risk of sounding redundant, I believe that taking the step of tuning out television for a month will radically sharpen the focus of your family.

But then again, maybe you're still undecided. It's possible you simply cannot conceive of a daily routine devoid of TV. As I reviewed the pre-turnoff surveys from the families who participated, I noticed that many of them had worried about such things as: "Where will I get my news and information? What about late-breaking weather bulletins? What will we do for entertainment? Won't we be b-o-r-e-d? The television keeps me company, so how will I feel connected to the rest of the world?"

I empathize with each of these concerns. The great news is that most—if not all—of these issues can be satisfied through the power of radio.

Okay. It's possible you might be a little suspicious of me, a former radio disc jockey taking a swipe at television. Better let me clear the air: Our family does, in fact, have a TV. Granted, it's bound and gagged and occupies a dark, musty corner of the basement next to the TV-shaped dartboard.

Seriously, before you tune me out, let me say that I hold that the *balanced* usage of TV is our ultimate goal. But most of our homes have been grossly erring on the side of excessive TV consumption for far too long. A little diet is in order to get our priorities back into place.

In this chapter it will be my privilege to provide you with a perspective of radio from the inside out. Along the way, I'll highlight several surprising benefits this medium offers over the typical TV-viewing experience. In the next chapter I'll make a few suggestions as to where you might start as you explore some of the classic material from the Golden Age of radio as well as a number of contemporary "classics."

Who knows? If you've been hesitating to take the challenge, these insights and ideas might just give you the confidence you need to give the turnoff a try. I certainly hope so. If you're ready, let's get started . . . and the best place, as they say, is always at the beginning.

WIRED FOR SOUND

My first radio wasn't a thing of beauty. Quite the contrary. It was a pathetic and yet promising piece of technology. I wish you could have seen the jumble of wires, vacuum tubes, and assorted electronic parts lying exposed to the elements on my bedroom floor. At the sight of it, you might have said, "Bob, have mercy—put that thing out of its misery!"

I, however, was twelve years old, and my restless junior high imagination danced with the possibilities of that old Zenith. I remember the day when I first carried the radio to my room. It didn't have a nice case to protect its internal organs. In fact, the speaker dangled precariously off to one side attached only by two slim wires. So with more care than skill, I pounded a few scraps of wood into a box-like case that served as home for the speaker.

I finished with the casing, and with a twist of the knob, the

Zenith slowly came to life. As I listened, I was fascinated with my radio's ability to reach across so many miles and enter a little bedroom as it did that evening.

Listening to those first few scratchy sounds, I had the bright idea of increasing its range with a really big antenna. I borrowed the "rabbit ears" antenna from our Philco TV set and did the best I could to connect it to my radio. That evening I stayed up in my room tuning across the dial, slowly picking up new stations. I could tell the signal was coming from a great distance as the sound flowed in and out like gentle waves on a sandy shore.

Chicago . . . Baltimore . . . St. Louis . . .

It would amaze me that I could be listening to a baseball game from Chicago or a news program in New York right there in my bedroom in Philadelphia. This would have been during the late sixties.

The thrill of discovering some distant station was soon replaced by my amazement at the skill of those who were communicating on the air. I was enthralled by their ability to grab the listeners and keep them tuned in. In fact, I found myself listening more to the announcers, the presenters, the on-air talent than to the music or other entertainment offered.

Of course, I was fascinated by the drama programs, as any youngster would be. But I was more caught up in the way these personalities could hold the audience. Listening to those gifted announcers for hours at a stretch was the way I first became attracted to getting involved in the medium myself. Little did I know that playing with that old Zenith radio as a child would become the first step in carving out my future as an on-air personality on stations in both Philadelphia and Pittsburgh.

LIGHTS, CAMERA, ACTION!

A bit of radio history is in order. Radio station KDKA began with regular programming out of Pittsburgh as one of the first commercial radio stations around 1920. At first people didn't think it would work. The naysayers asked how this newfangled device could be of any interest to the average person. But with the broadcasting of sports, the ability to provide instant election returns, and the creation of entertaining dramas, millions of families gathered around the "wireless" each night.

"I'd occasionally prefer to listen to the television rather than watch it."

Interestingly, when TV first came along in the late thirties, it didn't catch on. Listeners accustomed to using their minds were bored by television's lack of imagination. Back then TV had started with news programs. It simply mimicked radio. Producers literally took radio shows and put them on television. When they finally began to create things unique to TV, they were able to pull people away from the radio. But TV was still something you had to park yourself in front of. Also, programming was only on in the evenings with a limited schedule. AM radio continued to dominate the American home for many years.

Then FM radio came into its own in the sixties, boasting a clearer, cleaner sound. With Elvis and the Beatles and other changes in music, that generation gravitated toward the higher quality of FM radio for music. Automobiles were no longer outfitted with just a single-speaker AM radio mounted on the front dash. For an added price, FM stereo with two speakers became the sought-after option.

Television, meanwhile, started to rise in popularity with the addition of color. By the seventies the evenings became deserts for radio as everyone drifted to TV land.

In the eighties AM radio enjoyed a resurgence once they rediscovered the "talk" radio format. Some attribute this renewed interest to Rush Limbaugh. All of a sudden people were interested in politics, and they wanted to eavesdrop on what the experts had to say. Along the way, someone started to put callers on the air, actually a relatively new phenomenon.

While television may have won the tug-of-war with radio, in my opinion the consumer lost something special—the gift of imagination.

PICTURE THIS

There's an enormous difference between the way radio and TV tell a story. Simply put, radio (like reading) paints with ideas, and you supply the images as you follow along. In a very real sense, the listening experience is a partnership between you and the broadcaster.

By contrast, television provides *both* the ideas and the images, leaving little or no room for the imagination. Your experiences are not necessary for the story to take shape. In fact, when we watch TV, our minds enter a state of rest almost akin to sleep.

Let me illustrate this difference between the two mediums another way. You and I each have our own set of life experiences. Let's say I was going to describe a fall scene to you over the radio. I start with an image in my mind that perhaps takes me back to some very comfortable, warm, and friendly situation I was involved in many years ago in the fall. I will speak the words in a certain way that means something specific to me and to my mental picture.

For you, those same spoken words will bring a different picture into your mind, a picture based upon *your* experiences in life. In the end you'll have a different mental experience—one that is your very own.

That's the beauty of the theater of the mind. It not only communicates the same story, says the same words, begins in the same way, takes you through the same storyline, and ends with the same conclusion, but you experience it in a different way than I do, because your mind will overlay your own understanding and your own experiences with the story that's being told.

If I'm talking about a large city, a country setting, this old house, or an old tree fort—all of those images are colored in your mind by what you've experienced. As author Hallie Flanagan said during the dawn of radio, "The power of radio is not that it speaks to millions, but that it speaks intimately and privately to each one of those millions."

With television you put your own experiences aside. What you've seen and gone through is not necessarily a part of what you're now being told and what you're seeing. You're essentially being told what to think.

As a result, the theater of the mind is gone! There can still be a tremendous amount of emotion from the visual stimuli TV offers, but it's not something that causes your mind to work harder. You just sit there and take it in. You're no longer a participant, except that you're reacting to the series of prepackaged images parading before your stagnant eyes. You are not enjoying the story through an activated imagination. In short, you are primarily in a passive state.

"Television provides both the ideas and the images, leaving little or no room for the imagination."

Someone might argue that television is more colorful than radio at one level, due to the visual images. And yet on another deeper level, it's *less* colorful because your mind doesn't have the opportunity to do the work and think in new ways.

GET RADIO ACTIVE

There was an old phrase in radio during the fifties and sixties called "color radio." The expression was used among DJs on "top-40" radio. It meant to "paint pictures" for the audience. The announcers were encouraged to be colorful in their patter and their talk between the songs. They were challenged to say something that caused listeners' minds to go somewhere and experience something. That was a strength of the medium. TV was in color, but it couldn't do that—it couldn't send the imagination off in a fresh, original direction.

That's the unfortunate truth about television. TV tells us what to think and what to see—and that's it. Need proof? When you and I talk about a television program, we typically describe what we saw—how the program began and how it ended. But if we were to describe a story we've read or an old radio drama we've heard, we not only talk about the content, but we draw on our own experiences. We share what it reminded us of, how it took us back to some memory, what it felt like—we use those kinds of phrases when we talk about the theater of the mind.

Not so with television, especially since many of today's TV programs are devoid of creativity. I'm convinced that most viewers are looking for something new and fresh when they tune in. Yet night after night they leave disappointed because the "talent" takes the low road and panders to people's base instincts and interests. Instead of providing some wholesome creativity, they go to those taboo areas, constantly pushing the envelope.

"TV tells us what to think and what to see."

Am I right? Isn't that one of the primary reasons you're even reading this book? You're tired of the way television programs try to draw you in with titillation. Every once in a while something creative comes along, and it stands out. You say that's good, that's head and shoulders above the rest. Yet for the most part, we're left with a bitter aftertaste.

So what happened? Did viewers get lazy? Is the creative gene pool dried up?

Most of what we see on TV, sad to say, is commercially driven. It's developed with the bottom line in view. Management barks out the orders:

"We've got to do it as inexpensively as we can."

"We've got to do it as quickly as we can."

"And we've got to make as much money as we can."

"We've got to sell all of the commercials we can."

For obvious reasons, the easy way of accomplishing these mandates is to push the envelope on subject matter rather than explore the creative avenues and storylines that require more time and resources.

The net effect of this coarsening of our senses is a lack of patience with a storyline that doesn't include brawls, car chases, explosions, and special "wow" effects. Let me put it this way: An audience raised on Jerry Springer will have little patience for the pacing of Garrison Keillor's *Prairie Home Companion* on radio.

As a nation, we've traded away the subtle for the scandalous, the nuance for the outrageous. And I believe it's possible that we've been clubbed over the head for so long with shock material that it may just be too difficult to recover that lost sensibility.

What complicates the situation is that there's peer pressure to find out what everyone's talking about, even if it's not our cup of tea. So we get drawn into something we might not otherwise elect to watch. And then like any other addictive behavior, we get hooked. Before we know it, we're enjoying something we would have never been interested in before.

COBWEBS AND EARWAX

This state of affairs is why I'm convinced going TV-free for thirty days is such a fantastic idea. When we break free from the powerful TV-induced trance we provide room for our minds to get back to work.

"As a nation, we've traded away the subtle for the scandalous, the nuance for the outrageous."

We give our thoughts the room they need to roam. We permit fresh ideas to take root in the soil of a fertile imagination—one where we take control by providing our unique, God-given picture of reality.

I can't remember who said it, but a media critic once commented that the hours of TV-watching by nonreading children provide what is called alpha-level learning. The mind needn't make any pictures since the pictures are provided, so the mind cuts current as low as it can. I say it's time to pump up the power! Switch on our kids' imaginations by switching off the set.

Whether or not you ultimately decide to take the TV-turnoff challenge, do me a favor. Take time to explore the richness of radio. Allow your mind to experience true "living color."

Need help finding a place to start? Read on.

6

Rediscovering Radio

There are days when any electrical appliance in the house,
including the vacuum cleaner, seems to offer
more entertainment possibilities than the TV set.

HARRIET VAN HORNE[21]

A woman who was fascinated by the TV-turnoff idea dropped me this note: "I've been so addicted to television since I was a child that I can't imagine one day without it—not to mention thirty days! Send me the details, but I can't promise my family will cooperate in this venture."

I believe that a primary reason many folks "can't imagine one day without TV" is that they're stuck in the TV rut. On one hand, they've watched with dismay the steady decline in television broadcast standards. Night after night the steady stream of inappropriate material parades before the watchful eyes of their children. On the other hand, these folks feel powerless to do anything about it.

And it's quite possible they've overlooked radio as a worthy alternative for news, information, and entertainment. That's why in the previous chapter I took us through a brief study of the differences between the way TV and radio tell a story, as well as explaining the benefits of radio.

Radio, as you recall, invites us to use our unique experiences to supply the images as we listen. Unlike watching television, listening to radio unlocks the theater of our minds. In TV land we're provided with all the images, and so we are less actively involved in the entertainment process. What's more, radio for the most part doesn't push the boundaries of decency with the same zeal as many TV programs.

Speaking of radio's appeal to the theater of the mind, an interesting thing happened in Colorado Springs. In a bold move, a local Christian radio station, whose programming already included a lot of the talk format, recently experimented by airing a number of radio dramas from yesteryear. The management decided to feature about an hour or so each night of old-time radio drama from forty or fifty years ago rather than the usual lineup of teaching, preaching, and other traditional religious programs.

What prompted them to expand their format in this way? They discovered that these early radio shows actually fit in with the rest of their programming because the messages of shows back then were very wholesome. They didn't have the negative situations and behavior we see today—the sex, the violence, and whatever else today's creative elite think they need to present on television (and in some radio). It just wasn't part of the radio experience in the early days.

With the help of a company called When Radio Was (which syndicates radio dramas to several hundred broadcasters across the country), the station began airing these classics. Frankly, I'm not surprised that this move was a real hit with their listeners. In fact, it's become one of the most popular features on radio.

From where I sit, I see families and people of faith growing tired of entertainment that runs contrary to their value system. They've watched the standards of acceptable entertainment slip over the years, and they're hungry for interesting, creative, inspirational, educational, challenging, adventure-packed, wholesome entertainment. More than ever I'm convinced that programmers who can satisfy that hunger will find a vast audience of listeners (and viewers) craving those positive options.

In a moment I'll provide you with several praiseworthy radio options to use during your TV fast. But before I do, in case you're tempted to believe TV standards haven't slipped, I'd like to repeat a wonderful illustration Dr. James Dobson, President of Focus on the Family, uses to makes this point.

In the following graph, the top line represents a standard of acceptability for TV content held by the church thirty years ago. The bottom line represents what has been acceptable to many of those outside of the church (see illustration). Let's say you've been a Christian these last thirty years. What you would listen to, what you would read, what you would view has changed. And probably in most instances it has changed for the worse.

Think back twenty or thirty years to a time when you were offended by something on television. Maybe you didn't like what you saw, but for whatever reason, you waded through it. When you put up with the offensive language, off-color comment, or disrespectful attitude, that threshold of acceptability for you went down to a lower level (see top line).

STANDARD OF ACCEPTABILITY FOR TV CONTENT

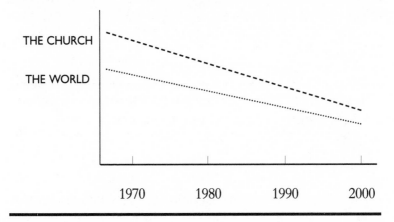

The same thing has happened in the world. Take, for example, the classics *I Love Lucy* and *The Dick Van Dyke Show*. Back then TV producers and script writers could not show a husband and wife in the same bed. Imagine that! A married couple had to be fully clothed in pajamas and in their own separate beds. Furthermore, when Lucy was pregnant, they had to say she was "with child" since "pregnant" was forbidden.

Today TV programs routinely show unmarried people in bed

engaged in various nonsleeping activities! In terms of dialogue, profanity peppers the salty conversations.

What's more, as the chart shows, these two lines have become closer together over time. The *difference* between what we in the church now accept and what the world accepts is not as great as it once was.

For the sake of argument, let's give it the benefit of a doubt and say that the two lines of acceptability are just as far apart today as they were thirty years ago. Even if that were true, what the world would accept without hesitation thirty years ago has become what the church will accept without hesitation today.

I believe the media is largely responsible for bringing us as a nation (both people inside and outside the church) down to this point. Some have called this shift the "dumbing down" of America. Others have referred to it as the "erosion of family values." Whatever the label, you and I live in a world that is "undistracted by a moral compass."

"The difference between what we in the church now accept and what the world accepts is not as great as it once was."

AT WIT'S END

It's one thing to point out these disturbing trends. It's quite another thing to do something about it. That's why Focus on the Family in Colorado Springs made a commitment to "light a candle" rather than just curse the darkness of this culture. I had the privilege of working for Focus on the Family for seven years and was thrilled when they announced the development of the *Adventures in Odyssey* radio drama for young people. It was first conceived back in 1986 and began as a once-a-week children's radio drama in 1987. It's now a thirty-minute feature heard daily around the world.

I recall Dr. Dobson decrying the fact that there just weren't many good children's radio drama options—at least not in Christian radio.

And so the creative team began to work on the *Adventures in Odyssey* series. I think everyone was surprised at how wildly successful it became almost overnight—for youth and their parents alike. My family wouldn't take a vacation without a stockpile of *Adventures* to accompany our driving! All these many years later, with several hundred episodes in the series, the cast of *Odyssey* has introduced a whole new generation to the power of the theater of the mind.

Over time the good folks at Focus on the Family realized that the *Adventures in Odyssey* audience had grown older and were in need of something new. Many of those early listeners now had children of their own. The Focus mailbag is frequently stuffed with letters from young adults who say they used to listen to *Odyssey*, and they are wondering what Focus has for them now. (Of course, there have always been those adults like myself who have enjoyed *Adventures in Odyssey*. We've gotten hooked on that stuff, so we're wanting the next thing, too.)

So on the heels of that first series' popularity, Focus developed the *Focus on the Family Radio Theater*. Designed for a little older listener, it's simply the same idea (using radio drama with its roots in the thirties and forties) but taking stories that are classic in their nature and presenting them in a full-blown radio drama format.

You'd be thrilled with the retelling of C. S. Lewis's entire Narnia series. I must admit their rendition of "Ben Hur" is nothing short of heart-pounding. Another wonderful dramatic presentation is "Bonhoeffer: The Cost of Freedom." And if you're doing your TV turnoff over the Christmas holidays, there's the unforgettable "A Christmas Carol" drama.

After all, there's nothing like a well-written story, a thick layer of sound effects, emotion-packed music, and a number of very talented actors and actresses to take you somewhere in your mind that allows you to be a vicarious participant through your own life experiences.

With the success they've experienced in radio drama, you might be wondering why more aren't entering the field of contemporary radio dramas for kids and family. Well, Disney has been working on producing some radio drama. And many of the radio stations that are airing the old stuff are doing very, very well with it. As much as I'd like to see them take it to the next level by creating some of their own programming, I'd be the first to recognize that to do it well can be relatively expensive.

At Focus, for instance, the cost to produce a three-hour radio production with custom music, top quality actors and actresses, and extremely high production values is well above a hundred thousand dollars, maybe even several hundred thousand dollars. For most radio stations, that's just not in the realm of possibility.

Even though they spend much less on each episode of *Odyssey*, somewhere in the neighborhood of $15,000 per half hour, that would still be a large investment for any radio station.

Another notable contribution to radio drama has been some of the fine work by the National Public Radio (NPR) network. Based upon their own press, the most popular thing NPR has ever aired is not Garrison Keillor's wildly successful *Prairie Home Companion*. It was their serialization into a radio drama format of the hit movie *Star Wars*. They had more listeners tuning in and generated more requests for the cassette tapes and CDs than for anything else they've done.

Granted, *Star Wars* has a huge following. And it's a fun story to begin with. But NPR artfully retold the whole George Lucas story and did a marvelous job of presenting it so that when you closed your eyes, you were transported to wherever they were. The use of sound effects was superb. The actors and actresses were first rate. So even in a TV-oriented society, NPR proved that the theater of the mind is still alive and well. That's why I think there's a great future for radio drama when it's done right.

By the way, if you seek out radio dramas created by the British Broadcasting Company (BBC) as well as programs produced in other countries, you'll find many more selections. A number of those countries have a larger portion of their population listening to radio than watching TV, and so they're using more creativity in what they produce.

LOONY TUNES

In addition to the *Focus on the Family Radio Theater* selections, there are literally hundreds of classic radio shows available on cassette tape or CD, which your family might want to explore during your TV-free month. Before I provide a few of those examples to get you started, let me highlight one other benefit of radio drama over today's modern television cartoons.

Part of the attraction of radio drama is that it's closer to real life than many, if not most, of today's action-figure cartoons on television. Listeners can imagine themselves in the midst of the action as it unfolds in these radio episodes. What's more, most of these stories contain a solid moral lesson.

By contrast, rarely are young people *connected* to the eye-stimulating entertainment action they see on Saturday morning cartoons. Viewers typically don't learn a lot from what they see. And if they do, frequently it's a negative message involving violence, greed, or disrespect for authority. The days of the good guys coming out on top in the end are history. Granted, there are exceptions, but by and large children today are presented with little in the way of socially redeeming images, plots, or characters in the cartoons they watch.

Programs such as *Odyssey* or the old-time radio dramas often present a positive moral lesson. The listener can learn something from the situations presented, be it the consequences of shoplifting or the way a "little" lie grows into a mountain of deception.

"The days of the good guys coming out on top in the end are history."

Much of television today, as you well know, takes the viewer into the bizarre seamy areas of life through titillation and violence. We're a long way from the morality presented in *Father Knows Best, Leave It to Beaver,* or even *The Andy Griffith Show.* In fact, you get criticized if you even talk about such programs! We're told those shows are not "real" in terms of what's going on in our lives today. I believe that's partially because so much of what has been pumped into our minds by the media elite over the years has taken us in the direction of these perversions.

PUMP UP THE VOLUME

I must confess that before I highlight a number of the "good old" radio dramas, I feel some hesitation. Why? I'm fully aware that if you rush out to listen to a number of the classic radio selections I'm about to propose, it's likely you'll find these programs a little slow-moving, especially when compared to what we're familiar with on television.

It's a fact. Today's TV shows are intentionally designed to put viewers into a constant state of hyperdrive. The action, the graphics, the music, the rapidly changing camera angles—all contribute to a frenetic viewing experience. Whether we know it or not, you and I have grown accustomed to this delirious level of "story pacing." Many action-packed shows resemble a mouse on steroids spinning his cage wheel at lightning speed—but going nowhere fast.

As such, when it comes to just about any form of entertainment, television in the twenty-first century has raised the bar of our expectations. If you've stayed at Motel 6, for example, you'll get a clean, no-frills place to sleep. If you upgraded your choice of hotel and made it a habit of sleeping in one of the Ritz Carlton's posh suites (which can cost upwards of $750 a night), you'd find going back to sleep at Motel 6 a real nightmare (pun intended)!

The same is true with the dynamic of moving from television back to radio. When you and I reach for a radio classic, it's possible that the content won't seem to be really "happening." Remember, it was created during a much calmer period in our history. That's why you've got to give the originality and personality of these radio classics time.

Furthermore, in half an hour of television programming, which we've all been weaned on, the costs continue to drive the creativity. What once was a half-hour program (which was really twenty-seven minutes with three minutes of commercials) is now maybe eighteen minutes of actual story content with eleven to twelve minutes of commercial time. Broadcasters are forced to sell more time to cover their expenses.

When I say that the cost of creating TV shows is high, I mean that it's much more expensive than radio. In fact, many prime-time programs cost more than $1.5 million for just one "thirty-minute" episode. To recoup their costs, the networks jam as many paid commercials into the program as possible. I just read an article saying that TV stations are now experimenting with a five-second commercial! They hope to attract the ".com" Internet advertiser with these mini-spots.

So in this environment, a producer of a TV show today must answer this question: "How do you tell your story in eighteen minutes?" First, he's got to skip over the slower parts and go from one eye-catching, ear-grabbing situation to another. Secondly, the producer must answer: "How do you make sure people hang in there between those three- and four-minute commercial breaks?" They've decided that the best solution is to move the content way out to the edge with some crazy cliff-hanger device. The producer is, by necessity, driven to featuring extremes. We, in turn, grow numb to those extremes and bizarre behavior.

"It's a fact. Today's TV shows are intentionally designed to put viewers into a constant state of hyperdrive."

By contrast, the cost of producing an hour of radio music and talk is much, much less. So the pressure to squeeze cash out of an hour of radio is not as great. And yet if you're a radio programmer in a hot market such as Los Angeles, New York, Chicago, Philadelphia, or Atlanta, you must figure out how to stay competitive. You don't do it with ho-hum, mundane "how are ya doing" conversations, but rather with the kind of "shock talk" that pushes the limits of propriety.

When they open up the phone lines, they put on the air only those folks who seem just a little off the wall, just a little off center, or they play the caller for laughs. The Howard Stern-type shock-jocks of the world are looking for a way to make a name for themselves. They resort to depravity just to suck listeners in. That's both wrong and an unfortunate by-product of our permissive society, which is why I keep going back to the treasures of yesteryear.

TUNING IN

I have a hunch. When I speak of old-time radio drama, you may be picturing Grandma sitting in a rocking chair doing needlepoint as she listens to radio. Further, you might wonder if these programs are really any good—or is Bob just being sentimental.

From a radio drama perspective, a lot of the old story lines can at times move slowly. And compared to today, the sound effects were rather lame. In some instances the audio quality is pretty weak, too. But keep in mind, many of these classic productions were recorded fifty or sixty years ago.

There are three kinds of radio drama productions. The first are the old classics rendered in their *original format*. These are the ones that sometimes fall into the "hokey" category. They're still interesting, but some require more "grace" from the modern listener.

The second kind of production is the *recreation* of these older shows. Take, for example, a production of the *Lux Radio Theater* that distills a classic into a one-hour format. Here you've got the power of the story itself to hold you, not to mention the incredible skill of the actors and actresses, plus improved sonic quality.

Here is a wide range of classic shows listed in alphabetical order:

Abbott and Costello	*I Love a Mystery*
Burns and Allen	*Jack Benny Show*
Captain Midnight	*Life of Riley*
Dick Tracy	*Lights Out*
Dragnet	*The Lone Ranger*
Ellery Queen	*Ozzie and Harriet*
Father Knows Best	*Perry Mason*

Fibber McGee and Molly	*The Shadow*
Fireside Theater	*Sherlock Holmes*
The Green Hornet	*The Six Shooter*
Gunsmoke	*Superman*
Hopalong Cassidy	*The Whistler*
House of Mystery	*X Minus One*

I'm not personally endorsing all of the content of these shows—primarily because I haven't had the opportunity to preview each of them. At the same time, I'm reasonably confident you'll find the majority of programs to be a source of wholesome entertainment.

And if you happen to be more computer literate than myself, you'll also discover that there are hundreds of web sites on the Internet where you can learn more about these selections on tape or CD. Some web sites permit you to sample a radio program via your computer's RealAudio Player.

Due to the rapid changes on the Internet, I won't list web sites. Any web address I provide today would likely change by the time you read my suggestions. The best approach would be to use a search engine to find key words such as "old-time radio drama," "classic radio showcase," *Lux Radio Theater, Suspense Radio Theater,* or "vintage radio." Each should provide a wealth of web sites for you and your family to explore.

At a local discount warehouse I happened to notice a number of worthy old-time radio collections on cassette tape. One example was *Old-Time Radio's Greatest Detectives,* which features sixty programs including "The Shadow," "Dragnet," "Johnny Dollar," and "Philip Marlowe." For around thirty dollars it's a great way to gain an introduction to some of the adventure and mystery classics.

Likewise, I found *The 60 Greatest Old-Time Radio Shows of the 20th Century.* This collection was assembled by Walter Cronkite and contains the must-have Abbott and Costello's "Who's on First." Your kids are sure to shake their heads in amazement over that routine. The collection also has Orson Welles's version of "War of the Worlds" plus selections from *Fibber McGee and Molly, Jack Benny,* and *Lights Out.* I also found anthologies of *Sherlock Holmes*, various Western thrillers, and a collection of other one-time broadcasts assembled by CBS.

The third kind of radio drama production I want to mention is represented by *contemporary creations* such as *Adventures in Odyssey*. These are first-class dramas that demonstrate how radio has grown up. These shows capitalize on the ability to use just audio to paint a dramatic picture of what's going on.

If you can't imagine going without television for a month, much like the woman whose letter I quoted at the beginning of this chapter, I trust that these ideas will provide you with a fresh alternative for entertainment in the days ahead as you rediscover radio. Oh, should you want to learn more about the *Focus on the Family Radio Theater* or *Adventures in Odyssey,* feel free to explore their web site at Family.org or call 1-800-AFAMILY.

As you turn off the TV for a month, I pray this will be a special time in your life and that of your family as together you fine-tune your imagination.

7

Journal the Journey

Don't you wish there were a knob on the TV
to turn up the intelligence?
There's one marked "Brightness," but it doesn't work.

GALLAGHER[22]

Have you ever gone white-water rafting?

I've "shot the rapids" in Colorado, Tennessee, and South Carolina, and I confess it's a blast! If you've never gone, here's the drill. You and your buddies start by selecting the proper life vests, helmets, and paddles. Then a seasoned trail guide explains what's ahead *before* you push off into the swirling waters. He or she helps you anticipate the unique challenges that a particular river will present—especially if the water level is low (which can introduce jaw-like rocks to your inflated raft).

Once you get on board, your guide demonstrates the proper use of your paddle to maneuver the raft. Throughout the run, this knowledgeable leader gives you an idea of what's "next." Frankly, I found it only partially comforting to be told that the next bend in the river had a "teapot" that we must avoid to prevent capsizing! Yet for the most part, the very fact that the trail guide had already been down the stream many times before—and survived—was reassuring.

PREVIEW OF COMING ATTRACTIONS

Just as my rafting captain provided me with a view of what was ahead, I thought you'd appreciate getting a feel for "what's ahead" when you take your TV-turnoff challenge. To that end, I've reprinted the journal from James and Debbie of Austin, Texas, whose experiences struck me as a perfect warm-up for those who may be wondering what it's actually like to go "cold turkey." In a moment you'll have the opportunity to be a fly on the wall of their home. But first here's a brief note they sent me along with their final journal:

September 1, 1999
Dear Bob,
  I copied our journal below. We, too, wondered what to do now that we've completed the fast. Actually, we came up with a solution very similar to the one you prescribed—we're going to allow TV on Friday and Saturday only.
  We did plug it back in today, and the kids were allowed one thirty-minute program. I was very sad to plug it in. It was so nice without it. Hopefully we have broken the habit of TV, and by limiting it to the weekends, we will not slide back into it ever again!!
  By the way, here's a look at our ages: James—39, Debbie—36, David—9, Emily—8, Brad—5.

DAY 1: SUNDAY, AUGUST 1

We started on a Sunday, which makes it easier as we don't allow TV-watching on Sunday mornings and afternoons. We do go to Grandmother's house every Sunday evening for dinner, and the kids (particularly David) are in the habit of watching the ABC Disney movie at her house. We explained what we were doing to the extended family, and they were very supportive. The kids played with their cousins instead of watching TV. When we got home, we read through the TV-turnoff rules and then discussed everyone's thoughts from the day:
  DAVID: I'm going to have to figure out something to do, or I'm going to mope around for a month. I agree with Mom that we need to do this. Because this seems so hard, it proves that we need to do it. We obviously need a break from TV if it is so hard to give it up for even one day.
  BRAD: I think that it's going to be good learning for us. I think I'm going to be kind of bored, but it will be good because I have those Legos to build with. I'm glad that I have a basketball hoop in my room. This is going to be really, really fun for Mom and Dad.

DEBBIE: *I'm not sure it's going to be so much fun. The constant refrains of "Why are we doing this?" and "I'm going to be soooo bored" are already wearing thin.*

Emily and James have no thoughts to share because Emily was very negative about the whole thing. In a very disrespectful tone of voice she said that if this was the decision her family wanted to make, she was officially no longer in our family; therefore, she is upstairs getting a bath and heading for bed.

While I was typing this in, Brad went into the playroom and pulled out an assortment of games and puzzles and laid them out on the floor. He was very pleased to show them to us, and James praised him for looking at the positive side and thinking of other things to do. After baths Emily had reformed her attitude, so we pulled out the cards and played a game.

DAYS 2-5: MONDAY, AUGUST 2—THURSDAY, AUGUST 5

We have a little confession: We planned our no-TV time for this month because we had already decided to spend this week at a lake in a cabin that did not have a TV. We went with four other families—ten adults and seventeen kids ages four to eleven. We had a fantastic time. The kids rode bikes, swam, rode on a boat, water-skied, fished, read books, searched out secret hideouts, listened to audio tapes, played games and cards, and had an all-around fantastic time.

I asked everyone how their week was without TV:

DAVID: *It was pretty easy since there was so much to do.*

EMILY: *The first week without TV has been pretty easy.*

BRAD: *It was fine with no TV. I didn't really miss it at all.*

JAMES: *As long as you go somewhere fun, you don't miss it much.*

DAY 6: FRIDAY, AUGUST 6

DEBBIE: *I was particularly dreading the afternoon when I would need to get unpacked and do laundry, and the kids would spend the time without TV or neighbor kids as an option. Much to my surprise, they did great! Brad and Emily spent quite a lot of time in their rooms. Emily played with her American Girl doll, and Bradley built with Legos. David entertained himself by reading, playing on the computer, and building with Legos.*

Later in the afternoon, at Emily's request, I retrieved an old box for her, and she and Bradley cut, taped, and decorated it until they had converted it into a spaceship. They then took turns taking space missions! I'm absolutely certain that would not have happened had I allowed them to watch TV.

One extra note: While at the lake, the kids' physical activity was greatly increased over the norm, and they slept much better and longer than they usually do. It struck me as a much healthier lifestyle than the life we usually lead where time each day is spent in front of the TV.

Again I asked the family how the day was without TV:

DAVID: *It's been pretty tough coming back because there doesn't seem to be much to do when we were used to a lot of stuff at the lake.*

EMILY: *Today was pretty easy because I had so many ideas from my vacation that I wanted to try out. But I'm still not sure about the rest of the month.*

BRAD: *It's been fine today.*

DEBBIE: *From my point of view, I think it looked like everyone was pretty busy except David. At one time he was reading a book. Well, that's pretty much it for today. I'll check back in later.*

DAY 7: SATURDAY, AUGUST 7

DEBBIE: *Our first Saturday without Saturday morning cartoons. The house was nice and quiet for the morning, which I really enjoyed. Having the TV on in the morning is one of my least favorite things.*

JAMES: *It was a little quiet on Saturday morning, and that was different, but it was okay.*

DAVID: *It was okay because I can still play the computer.*

EMILY: *I didn't like it very much. I missed the cartoons.*

BRAD: *It was good because we've already seen all of them.*

Last week David, Emily, and Brad asked their grandfather how he spent his time when he was a child (before TV), and he told them he spent a lot more time outdoors. He listed the games he and his friends used to play and the hours they spent creating new activities, like the time they gathered up all the old Christmas trees and made a huge fort by stacking the trees in piles.

DAY 8: SUNDAY, AUGUST 8

Once again, not watching TV at Grandmother's house was not a problem. One particularly wonderful thing came out of this. David usually sits in front of the TV most of the time we are there, rarely interacting with his cousins. Tonight he played with his two younger cousins. He had a wonderful time hiding and jumping out and surprising them. Afterward he commented several times what fun it was to hear them squeal with delight.

It's scary to realize that the TV has been robbing them of a relationship with each other. If the other families will go for it, I am hopeful that we will make the TV turnoff at Grandmother's house a permanent change.

James and I had a date this evening, so we allowed the kids to rent and watch A Kid in King Arthur's Court *with the baby-sitter. It went well, and they really enjoyed it. There were TV screens on at the video store with Nintendo games on them, and the boys spent five minutes at the store playing them before we reminded them that they weren't supposed to be doing that. They were both surprised to realize that they had started playing without even thinking about it.*

DAY 9: MONDAY, AUGUST 9

DEBBIE: *I am really enjoying TV-free mornings. The house is so much more peaceful without it. We have never turned it on in the mornings on school days, and I remember now why we established that rule. I had planned to spend a lot of time with the kids at the pool this last week of David's and Emily's summer vacation, but unfortunately David has swimmer's ear. I am not sure how we will spend our time now.*

We do have back-to-school sleepovers planned at our house for Emily and her friends on Wednesday evening and for David and his friends on Thursday evening. Our usual activity for those evenings would be a movie or Nintendo, so we are going to have to give a little more thought to activities. We are tentatively planning on game nights!

Emily is really making incredibly good use of her time without the TV. Saturday she pulled out a clay book and made a clay mouse and clothing for the mouse. Yesterday she pulled out an origami book, and she has made several interesting creations with it. This is mildly amusing because she complained the loudest at first about giving up the TV.

David is still spending large amounts of time in front of the computer screen, but I am going to put limits on that today, so we will see what he then does with his time.

Brad is spending a little time on the computer and more time building with Legos and playing with Emily. He asks us to play with him more, which is fun if I remember that my housework is not urgent and playing with him is. He starts kindergarten in two weeks!

Evening notes from **DEBBIE**: This is the first evening that I would like to watch TV. It has been a long, tedious day of running errands and housework, and I would love to just sit and watch the news. As a general rule, James and I make time to sit and visit with each other each evening, and we often end the evening watching the news and then see either a little Leno or Letterman. It is a nice way to finish the day, sitting together on the couch, drinking coffee, and unwinding together.

DAY 10: TUESDAY, AUGUST 10

What a treat! I came downstairs this morning, and all three kids were sitting on the living room floor playing a card game together instead of sitting glassy-eyed in front of the TV.

In the afternoon I took the kids to get haircuts at a salon that caters to children. Each styling chair faces a TV screen, and they continually play Disney movies. It would have been impossible for the kids to avoid watching the TV, and I didn't want to take them somewhere else, so I gave them permission to watch it and promised I would record that they couldn't avoid it.

DAY 11: WEDNESDAY, AUGUST 11

The kids spent the morning tying each other to a chair and seeing how long it took them to work free of the ropes—a little Houdini act. In the afternoon they all three played together, building with K'nex and Legos. David realized that he had a K'nex motor that he could connect to his K'nex robot and make the robot's head spin at a high rate of speed. With Brad and Emily's help, they connected a Lego chain to the robot's head and then suspended Lego men from the chain to see how many Lego men could be spun at once before the robot would wobble enough to fall over.

They had a wonderful time, played great together, and had fun experimenting. As a general rule, they play together very well without the TV. It's amazing to see how much more time they spend playing, imagining, creating, and interacting with each other.

David commented today that he is getting used to no TV and thinks he is finding interesting things to do. The kids also noticed the television sets at Target and had a difficult time ignoring them while we shopped.

Emily's sleepover went just fine without TV. We swam at the lake (close to home), made ice cream sundaes, painted fingernails, fixed hair, and danced to loud music.

DAY 12: THURSDAY, AUGUST 12

Today without the TV was fine. This morning Emily and her girlfriends made ankle bracelets for each other and played with Beanie Babies instead of watching TV.

It is late at night, and I find myself once again missing the TV as an unwinding tool. David has four nine- and ten-year-old boys here for a sleepover, and while they are adorable, fun, and silly, they wear me out. I would love to sit on the couch and veg out in front of the tube. I doubt the boys will play as well and as quietly tomorrow morning as the girls did this morning. The TV is often useful to keep the boys from running through the house. They have so much energy.

I am very glad we are doing this because the kids are enjoying each other immensely. Their imaginations seem to feed each other's. When one child comes up with an inventive idea, the other two will build on it. It is a treat to watch. Also I spend more time visiting with them, which is great! I am realizing more and more that the TV is a thief, not just of time but of relationships.

David, Emily, and Brad are going to spend the night tomorrow at a good friend's house. The friends know we are avoiding TV for a month, but I am hesitant to ask them to enforce it at their house because I know it does mean more work for the parents. It will be interesting to see how it goes.

DAY 14: SATURDAY, AUGUST 14

I told David, Emily, and Brad that the choice of whether or not to watch TV while spending the night out was up to them. I encouraged them to try to find *something else to do, but I didn't want their hosts to have to adjust their plans to accommodate our no-TV commitment. They did end up watching a thirty-minute program yesterday and a thirty-minute program this morning, and David played Nintendo with his friend.*

James and I agree that so far we are really enjoying no TV. It is not as hard as we had anticipated, the kids are not mopey or bored, which we had anticipated, and the up side has been a nice, quiet household with more interaction.

DAY 16: MONDAY, AUGUST 16

Today was the first day of school for David and Emily, and the house was very quiet. I caught myself heading to turn on the TV twice just because I wanted the noise to fill the house and distract me from missing them, but not because I wanted to watch TV. I had anticipated that this week and next week would be the most difficult without TV for me. This week Brad is still home, but next week he starts kindergarten. I will be home for long stretches by myself for the first time in ten years. I have been dreading the quiet for a long time, and I will not have the TV to drown out the silence and distract me from the loneliness.

I was willing to go without the TV during this difficult transition because I felt certain that I could depend on the Lord to fill in the silence, but I must admit that I am dreading it. I am not one of those mommies who celebrates when the kids are back in school. Next to my husband, my kids are my favorite people, and I love being with them.

DAY 19: THURSDAY, AUGUST 19

What an unbelievable blessing it has been not to have the TV on this week! It is Brad's last week before starting kindergarten, and because David and Emily are already in school, he has a lot of time to fill. Instead of using the TV, I have put down my chores for the week, only doing what is absolutely necessary, and have spent the hours reading to him, playing hide-and-seek with him, playing games with him, and enjoying him.

This is a priceless gift. I know I would have made extra effort to spend more time with him this week even with the TV on, but I still would have ended the week with regrets about not making the most of the time because I would have filled hours each day with chores while he watched TV. Thank you.

Another funny thing has happened. I am usually a night owl and rarely get enough sleep. During the school year I would often run out of steam by midafternoon and would use the kid's after-school TV time to catch a quick nap.

Now without the TV perpetually on, I find myself going to bed about an hour earlier each night, and therefore I'm not nearly so tired late in the day. I used to think I needed the TV on after school so that I could have down time. Now I realize I just need more sleep, and I have the energy to give my kids the attention they need and deserve when they arrive home from school instead of being exhausted and desperate for a nap or caffeine!

A couple more realizations: When James and I did sit on the couch watching TV at night, he would usually rub my shoulders, or we would sit close. I do miss that regular physical closeness each day, and I'm not sure how to add that back in on a regular basis.

Last observation: Without the TV I am very uninformed about world news. I do read the newspapers on-line every other day or so, but I still feel very removed from world events. This has been mostly positive. I think I often tend to waste a lot of time focused on the news, and this can be a thief of joy and leave you feeling depressed.

For example, watching the continuous coverage of JFK, Jr.'s death last month was incredibly depressing. Had I been able to watch TV this week, I'm sure I would have spent a lot of time immersed in the tragedy of the earthquake in Turkey. I would have watched the news footage of the rescues of survivors and of the pictures of the dead, and I would have listened when the journalists interviewed the grieving people who had lost family members. It would have been incredibly sad and hopeless.

Because I have not had the TV on, I only became aware of the earthquake when a friend mentioned it to me. I have now read two articles about it on-line, and I have seen the headlines announcing the incredible loss of life. As a result I have prayed more about this situation. Instead of just watching in horror and sadness and being overwhelmed by the pain of so many people, I have prayed, and then I have set those concerns down and have gone about the business that God has put before me today.

DAY 20: FRIDAY, AUGUST 20

Tonight my two nieces are coming to spend the night. We considered allowing the kids to rent a movie and watch it with them, but we decided we would rather that they enjoy each other and play instead. We took them swimming and then to a lakeside restaurant for dinner.

DAY 21: SATURDAY, AUGUST 21

The kids spent the night at their cousins' house, and they watched a movie there. It is striking how quickly we use a movie to entertain kids instead of planning alternate activities. I know I usually resort to this choice first because it is quick and easy and popular.

DAY 22: SUNDAY, AUGUST 22

We went to our brother and sister-in-law's house for dinner this evening to celebrate a birthday. I was wishing for TV for the kids as they ran through the house, often at full volume. It required repeatedly asking them to settle down. Unfortunately it is too hot to send them outdoors for long periods of time, although we did send them out for a while. It was difficult to enjoy adult conversation and a peaceful meal.

In addition, a hurricane hit the Texas coast this afternoon, and I found the information I could get on the Internet to be very limited. My sister-in-law did turn on the weather channel while we were there, and in three minutes I got more information on the storm than in thirty minutes of surfing the web. Apparently Internet news sources are severely reduced on Sundays.

DAY 24: TUESDAY, AUGUST 24

Now that all the kids are back in school, I took up exercising again this morning. I was on the treadmill and had been watching TV for fifteen minutes before I realized what I was doing. I unplugged the headphones and read for the remainder of my time. I had to tell the kids about it, but I told them that we had all committed to go without TV, so I would avoid it while I exercised for the rest of the week.

DAY 27: FRIDAY, AUGUST 27

I read a book while I exercised today, and it was fine. The time actually went more quickly, and I was less focused on the discomforts of exercise while reading than while watching TV.

I had written previously that I was worried about how this week would be without TV for noise and distraction while I'm alone since my youngest started kindergarten on Monday. I have not missed TV at all. I have simply been too busy, and I am so out of the habit of watching it that it has not occurred to me to miss it.

DAY 30: MONDAY, AUGUST 30

Final thoughts from the family:

DAVID: *Yahoo, it's finally over. I learned that the TV is hard to avoid at first, but then you get used to it. I'm happy with how I spent my time; I made a lot of progress on my Gameboy.*

EMILY: *Although it was difficult at first, I think that it's a lot easier now because it's easier to walk past the TV and not even notice it. I liked spending time with my friends and family, and I liked playing school, and I enjoyed homework more and got it done easier and more quickly. It was easier because I didn't need to rush to get it finished so that I could watch TV.*

Giving it up doesn't give me the uneasy feeling that it used to. It's hard to avoid TV at friends' houses, and I want to watch it even though I know I shouldn't. I got to do more things that I like, to notice the things around me, like my brothers and how they are growing up, and to encourage my little brother who just started kindergarten.

BRAD: *I think the TV-free month was very, very fun. It didn't feel much different. TV is kind of boring, so I'm only sort of looking forward to watching it again. It makes me grumpy. (At this point Brad turned to his sister and said, "Hey, Emily, let's play," and he ran off!)*

JAMES: *What a gift the past thirty days have been! Battles over the TV being on or on what channel have been eliminated, stronger channels of communication and cooperation have developed, and we're engaging our brains more! From card games to books to puppet shows to charades and Pictionary, we engage and* appreciate each other rather than poring over the TV schedule in search of that next great show.

As a parent, I have appreciated the precipitous drop in the requests for fast food, small plastic toys, and the latest breakfast cereals. As an adult, it has been refreshing to remain relatively unaffected by the media crisis du jour. For example, the tragic earthquake in Turkey happened two weeks ago. This has caused me to pray for those people and that country and reflect on God's providence in the face of such suffering.

But previously, in our usual TV mode, much of my prayer and reflection would have been replaced by nightly news shows and special reports on the tragedy, and my active prayer and contemplation would have been replaced by passive absorption of the latest video footage and reports from the scene. For me, the TV tends to dull my senses and my sensitivity to both the world and the people around me.

DEBBIE: Over the course of the month, I had two or three times when I missed the TV, and each time it was for a brief time after a stressful day when I just wanted to sit and do nothing. The other 719 hours since we turned the TV off have been fantastic. I thought that James and I would probably take advantage of the once-a-week movie option, but we haven't. We have allowed the kids to do that when they had a baby-sitter or stayed with a friend, but even that only happened three times in the month.

James and I have loved the TV being off so much that we have toyed with the idea of making it permanent. We have decided that, rather than outlawing it totally, we are going to limit TV-watching to Friday after school and on Saturday. If we find it is a problem for that short amount of time, we are still reserving the option to do away with it all together. I must confess, however, that I am not looking forward to turning it back on. I love the quiet!

"'For me, the TV tends to dull my senses and my sensitivity to both the world and the people around me.'"

One assumption we have always made is that in order for our house to be popular with kids through the teenage years, we would need a TV—and a big screen TV at that. The nights we had kids over for back-to-school sleepovers *have really made us rethink that assumption. The kids loved being here and will want to come back because it was fun, and we took the time to talk to them.*

Instead of thinking that we had to have entertainment to draw kids here in years to come, I have been reminded that what is really attractive is a place they feel welcome and cared for. A big plate of cookies, a warm welcome, attention, and a family that talks to each other will always be attractive to teenagers. Thank you for allowing us to participate in the thirty-day experiment. We have been blessed incredibly by it!!

DEAR DIARY

In order to maximize your TV-free experience, you'll find it beneficial to keep an ongoing journal of the challenges, discoveries, and obstacles you experience this month. Not a writer? No problem. This doesn't have to be fancy. You could, as Jennifer did, use a yellow legal pad with "Day One" written across the top of page one and so on. Scribbling notes on a wall calendar works, too.

The key is to jot down anything that caught you by surprise or that happened as a result of this decision to live without the television. Throughout the month, make note of the interesting reactions when you told your friends about the TV fast.

How did you handle a visit to a relative's home where they make use of television?

How did you navigate the no-TV commitment when your young person planned to go to a sleepover at a friend's home where TV is used to heat their house?

Look for insightful observations by the children. Notice their behavior. Did it take awhile for them to warm up to alternative activities? Did they mope around for days in a daze?

It would be wonderful if you encouraged your children to keep a journal, too. Have them either report to you how they're doing without TV (if they're too young to write), or provide them with an inexpensive binder in which they can keep an account of the TV-free experience in their own words. You could invite them to make notes and observations about how you're handling it!

At the end of the journey, you'll have a fantastic record of this watershed moment in the life of your family. Months, even years later you'll have a permanent narrative of the blessings and changes your family experienced.

Need a place to start? At the end of the first day, write a short description of what happened. Think about what it felt like. Was it difficult? Quiet? Lonely? Or easier than you imagined? Be sure to note what you did with the time instead of viewing TV during the first day.

"Encourage your children to keep a journal, too."

For example, Paul from Chicago, Illinois, noted, "The first night of our TV turnoff my wife, Pamela, and I sat on opposite sides of the couch in silence. It's funny. We didn't know what to say! We'd only been married for two years, but that evening we suddenly discovered that the TV had already replaced our meaningful dialogue." He adds, "We looked at each other and asked, 'Now what?'"

One last thing. If you'd like to send me a copy of your journal, I'd love to see it (address at the end of this book). Who knows? I may write a sequel to this book. I might feature your reflections!

WELCOME ABOARD!

Are you ready to set sail on this adventure? Great!

Tomorrow will be your first day of experiencing life without the TV. I'm confident that you can do it!

Sure, there will be no Barney.

No Energizer Bunny. No soaps.

No channel-surfing. No problem . . .

How can I be so confident? As you and your family launch out into uncharted, potentially shark-infested waters, I know the Lord will be there to strengthen your resolve. And the design of this book is a thirty-day supply of short, thought-provoking insights to accompany you on this journey. The chapter for each day will deal in a simple manner with our relationship to the tube from a biblical perspective.

So rather than reading ahead through the next thirty chapters now, take them one day at a time. You might consider reading a chapter after dinner as you linger over dessert. (Remember, there's no need to rush through the meal in order to catch a show. You're free to taste and enjoy Mom's cooking.) At the end of each insight I've included several questions to stimulate family discussion.

And don't underestimate the power of prayer. In fact, why not start right now to pray together as a family for the Lord to bless your undertaking. Ask Him to give you the strength to overcome any apprehension or obstacle that might hamper your success. In the words of King David, "Cast your cares on the LORD and he will sustain you; he will never let the righteous fall" (Psalm 55:22).

Oh, if you haven't done so yet, now is the perfect time to cart those TV sets into the basement or garage. Or, at the very least, unplug them. After you hide the remote controls find a bed sheet, tablecloth, or canvas to drape over each TV. Then dust off the games, books, magazines, toys, watercolors, sports equipment, and radios. Pull out those favorite tapes and CDs. And get ready for the time of your life!

PART TWO

And Now a Word from Our Sponsor

Guard Your Heart

Above all else, guard your heart,
for it is the wellspring of life.

PROVERBS 4:23

I'll never forget the day the President of the United States came to my office.

Well, not exactly *my* specific office space.

More like our office building.

It was 1992, and President George H. Bush was campaigning to get reelected for a second term. I was working for Focus on the Family in Colorado Springs at the time. President Bush was scheduled to discuss his position on various family issues with Dr. James Dobson for an upcoming radio broadcast.

Pretty neat stuff.

Imagine getting an announcement that the President of the United States would be arriving at your home. I guarantee it would be nothing short of electrifying.

The recording studio was in our building (we had six different buildings at the time). A memo was circulated describing the security measures required of all employees at our location.

Unlock all cabinets, closets, desks, and file drawers.

Any area not accessible would be crowbarred open to accommodate a pack of specially trained bomb-sniffing dogs. Once searched, that area was sealed off until the President concluded his visit.

Forget the employee parking lot. Anyone leaving his or her car would find it towed. Besides, we were told to stay home. The office would be closed for the day.

In fact, dozens of Colorado Springs police officers shut down several adjacent streets to all traffic. Bomb dogs sniffed the sewers, public trash cans, and sidewalk planters, anywhere an explosive device might be planted.

As if these precautions weren't enough, a tent was erected adjacent to the entrance.

A tent?

Yes. The presidential limousine would park its long, sleek, bullet-proof body inside this covering to prevent an enemy sharpshooter from having a view of the President exiting and reentering his limo.

These guys think of everything.

Although not in the memo, I later learned that Secret Service agents were posted on the rooftops of several nearby office buildings for added security.

The moment of truth came. I stood across the street with hundreds of other lookie-loos behind yellow police tape to catch a glimpse of our Fearless Leader.

At first the distant hum sounded like a squadron of bees buzzing their way toward us. Within moments the street began to vibrate as a caravan of police motorcycles flanking the presidential limo roared down main street into our headquarters. Several dark Suburbans, probably filled with Secret Service agents armed with machine guns, brought up the rear.

All of these measures were undertaken to do one thing—guard the President.

Seems like they went to a lot of trouble, not to mention expense, right? (I heard some estimates that placed the cost of these security measures in the neighborhood of $100,000.)

But isn't that what we do with the things we value most— whether it's the President of the most powerful country on the planet or just my puny savings account at the local bank. As a society, we guard what we perceive to be of great value.

King Solomon knew something about the use of guards. After all, he was one of the wealthiest kings who ever lived. According to the biblical account in 1 Kings 10:27a, "The king made silver as common in Jerusalem as stones." And yet look at Solomon's surprising advice: "Above all else, guard your heart."

Excuse me? My heart?

Why didn't he say, "Above all else, guard your *cash*"?

Because Solomon understood this secret: Our hearts possess the wellspring of life. When Solomon speaks of my heart, he's not talking about that beating pound of flesh within my chest.

My heart is the core of my being. It's the essence of who I am. It's where my mind and will, my emotions and convictions come together to shape what I believe and the choices I make.

When it comes to the heart, what are we guarding against? Who or what is the enemy? For people of faith, I believe one of the primary enemies is endless, indiscriminate TV-viewing. Why? Indiscriminate TV consumption opens the door behind which lives a three-headed monster called Distraction, Deception, and Division.

Let's take a quick look at each one.

Distraction promises me a fast-paced, thrill-a-minute experience of fun and excitement but ultimately prevents me from going deeper in my relationships with my family, my friends, and most importantly with God. Who has time for meaningful heart-to-heart conversation when TV does all of the talking?

Deception is a clever fellow because he seduces me into accepting something I otherwise know to be wrong, harmful—even deadly. For instance, my loving heavenly Father tells me to prize sex so highly that I must wait until I'm married to unwrap that divine gift. If, however, I let down my guard and stare at beautiful people in TV land bed-hopping night after night, I may begin to believe sex outside of marriage is okay since "everyone is doing it."

Division cuts to the center of my affections. It dangles the temptation of acquiring endless "stuff" with such dazzling appeal that I can easily forget the voice of my First Love who encourages me to "seek first the kingdom." If I'm not careful to guard against it, the charms of this world—fast cars, big houses, designer clothes, and the like— will consume me.

Today as you begin your TV-free month, why not take a few

moments to evaluate your security system. What steps have you taken to guard your heart?

BUT WAIT, THERE'S MORE!

1. Describe a time when television distracted you from having a meaningful conversation with a loved one.

2. The "views expressed" in many TV shows and advertisements could deceive us into believing something contrary to what the Bible teaches. Can you think of an example?

3. In Revelation 2:4 God told the believers in Ephesus, "Yet I hold this against you: You have forsaken your first love." What is the best way to maintain a tender, undivided heart toward the Savior?

You Are Dismissed

Back in college we nicknamed a particular professor "Dr. Snooze." We weren't trying to be mean. The fact of the matter was, his mono- tone drone sent our eyelids southward. Naturally, one of our favorite things to hear from him was "Class dismissed," especially if it was another one of his unmemorable late-night lectures.

Whether it's a boring business meeting with diminishing returns, a tired speech by an unprepared guest speaker at the PTA meeting, a sleepy sermon, or a wedding we were obligated to attend, my favorite thing to hear is . . .

"You are dismissed."

"Meeting adjourned."

"That's all for now."

After all, isn't that the way it is in "real life"? Every activity even- tually comes to a close. There's an end to the baseball game. There's an end to the work day and school day. Meetings, conversations, and phone calls all have a logical ending point. Stuff ends.

There's one exception to this rule.

Television-viewing.

Have you ever heard messages on TV such as: "You are dis- missed." "Go stretch your legs." "Turn us off and get some exercise." Or how about, "You've already spent too much time in that chair. Get up and do something meaningful!" No way. In TV land there's no end to the viewing.

Wait a minute, Bob! Don't shows come to an "end" every thirty or sixty minutes or so?

Sure. But take a closer look. What kind of messages do the networks lace throughout those thirty or sixty minutes of regularly scheduled programming?

"Stay tuned!"

"Tonight on Letterman, don't miss the amazing Joe Rock Star."

"But wait, there's more ahead."

"Up next—the shocking story of blah, blah, which you need to know. Details at 11:00!"

I guarantee that no network executive worth his salt would ever encourage a viewer to abandon his post, to turn off the tube and do something else.

Never. *Nunca.* Ain't gonna happen.

In fact, should you dare to think for yourself, for every reason you have to turn off the television, they'll provide ten compelling reasons to stay plugged in.

This fact has concerned even the U.S. Surgeon General. In April of 1999 Surgeon General David Satcher urged parents to take control of television consumption by reducing the time children spend staring at it. Why should he care? He's a doctor, not a psychologist.

Satcher noted in a press release that obesity levels had reached "epidemic proportions" primarily due to poor diet and a lack of physical activity. He observed, "We have the most sedentary generation of young people in American history. The percentage of overweight children has doubled since 1968."

So committed to stimulating real-life experiences and physical activity, he created a special booklet entitled, "Surgeon General's Prescription for Less TV." In it Satcher recommends that both children and parents "go bicycling, play soccer, jump rope, fly a kite, dance, start a garden, wash the dog, swim laps, throw a Frisbee, build a fort, learn to roller-skate . . ."

In short, anything that gets people out of their La-Z-Boys and into the heartbeat of life would be an improvement. He even suggests to kids: "Clean your room." Bottom line, Satcher believes Americans must cut their viewing by at least 50 percent if trends in obesity are to be reduced.

But there's a deeper issue. In today's psalm Moses invites the Lord to "teach us to number our days." Why? So we may "gain a heart of wisdom." To do what? Maximize the days God grants us.

In other words, life is short.

Life is far too precious to waste.

Moses wanted to stay focused on what *really* matters.

Since this fact has escaped the evening news, let me say what they'll never utter: "You are dismissed! You may now turn off the TV. You are free to go."

BUT WAIT, THERE'S MORE!

1. If you knew you only had a few months to live, how would you spend your time? What's stopping you from going for these activities now?

2. Furthermore, how high on your list of priorities would watching the latest episodes of a particular TV show be for you compared to other real-life options?

3. I'd be the first to acknowledge that some selective television viewing is appropriate. At the same time, how much is enough?

Know Your Stuff

As they led him away, they seized Simon from Cyrene,
who was on his way in from the country, and put the cross
on him and made him carry it behind Jesus.

LUKE 23:26

Something rather amazing happens to television around Easter. The networks "get religion" and resurrect a number of Easter classics. As a kid, I remember watching the Passion story where Christ was pictured nearly crushed under the weight of His cross. He staggered as He tried to ascend a cold stone stairway to the place of crucifixion, Golgotha.

It was a powerful scene.

The crowd wailed in anguish.

The mother of Jesus and His disciples were held back by the heavily armed Roman soldiers who remained unmoved by this display of human misery.

Suddenly, the dirty, tear-stained face of Jesus looked up at the camera. It was as if His eyes penetrated my TV set and locked their focus directly on me. At that moment the Hoover Dam couldn't prevent my tears from flowing. I felt helpless as the crown of thorns was pressed down upon Jesus' head, further into his blood-soaked brow.

Just when it looked as if Jesus couldn't muster the strength to take another step, I watched as Simon of Cyrene stepped in to shoulder the cross for Christ.

I remember thinking, *Simon—what a man!*

So unselfish.

So courageous.

So, well, so loving to come to the aid of Jesus.

I sat thinking how much I wanted a heart like Simon's.

Years later, while reading the account of the crucifixion in Luke 23, I paused at verse 26. We're told that a man was passing through town that day. Luke reports that "they *seized* Simon from Cyrene . . . and put the cross on him and *made* him carry it behind Jesus" (emphasis added).

Seized?

I thought he volunteered. Why, in the television movie . . .

Turning to Mark 15:21, I learned that Simon "was passing by," and "they *forced* him to carry the cross." And, like Mark's account, Matthew 27:32 records that "they *forced* him to carry the cross."

All of a sudden, I was forced to rethink my understanding of Simon's role during the crucifixion.

Why didn't Simon offer?

In fact, why did he *resist* carrying the cross?

Why wasn't Hollywood accurate when reenacting the story?

And—more importantly—what else might I be accepting as true just because I saw it on TV or in a movie?

How about you? Have you ever gotten the story mixed up because of what you've seen on television? Take, for example, the Christmas story. Many of the TV Christmas specials present a view of the manger scene with Mary, Joseph, the baby Jesus surrounded by animals, the shepherds, the Magi, and occasionally an angel hovering overhead.

Guess what? Contrary to this warm, fuzzy Kodak moment, the shepherds and the Magi were not at the manger at the same time. Sorry to burst your holiday bubble.

Or take that delightful animated movie *The Prince of Egypt.* Dreamworks Pictures worked hard to follow the biblical account. Even so, their version portrays a young Moses "accidentally" killing an Egyptian, prompting Moses to make a hasty exodus from the palace. Look at what the Scriptures say in Exodus 2:12: "Glancing this way and that and seeing no one, he *killed* the Egyptian and hid him in the sand" (emphasis added). This was no accident.

Again, consider Hollywood's view of history. In spite of a massive budget, the popular film *Titanic*, according to some responsible critics who read the actual ship logs, assert that the producers actually rewrote history. The film made the point that the rich first-class passengers were morally less upright in their behavior than those second- and third-class passengers. While people rushed to get into lifeboats, according to the film, the wealthy bribed their way onto a lifeboat. The ships logs do not support this view. In reality, the women and children got the first seats.

While television documentaries frequently do a commendable job of presenting history without homogenizing the facts, far too often a producer's bias is presented as fact.

Someone once said that if you repeat a lie often enough, it begins to sound like the truth. When it comes to our TV diet, that, my friend, is precisely why you and I must know the truth—not some Hollywood version of it.

BUT WAIT, THERE'S MORE!

1. Why do you think writers and producers change history when it would be just as easy to report the facts?

2. How might your personal study of Scripture help you to pinpoint falsehood in films and TV?

Cultivating Contentment

I know what it is to be in need, and I know what it is to have plenty.
I have learned the secret of being content in any and every situation,
whether well fed or hungry, whether living in plenty or in want.

PHILIPPIANS 4:12

A gentleman living in Muskogee, Oklahoma, wrote and asked Ann Landers her opinion about his favorite car—a 1937 Dodge, to be exact. He said he loved this car so much he wondered whether he could be buried in it instead of in a casket. He claimed it provided so many wonderful memories, he wanted to be "sitting at the wheel and lowered into the ground."[1]

Have you ever fallen in love with a car? I have.

In 1993 I purchased a Nissan Pathfinder. That would be the 4x4 SE version in a bold, bright Aztec Red. Complete with all the bells and whistles. Power everything. Alarm. Remote keyless entry. The sunroof and adjustable roof rack topped off this off-road dream machine.

Did I mention the shiny chrome bumpers?

The tires were "knee deep in tread." I'm talking big, road-hungry tires capable of swallowing the highest mountain in one bite.

The CD and tape player package was part of what the dealer called a "Premium" six-speaker sound system. Forget about the element of surprise—people would hear me coming two blocks before I arrived, thanks to that monster stereo.

Best of all, I knew the dealer. A personal friend of a friend. He worked the numbers and gave me a sweetheart of a deal on this low-mileage demo. I signed on the dotted line.

Payments for sixty months? For a ride like this? No problem. Big Red was destined to be the envy of my block.

Weekends I'd find a buddy to go "four-wheeling" up to the summit at Pike's Peak in the Rocky Mountains. And since I was single at the time, I enjoyed taking my date for a picnic somewhere on the mountainside. One woman I dated referred to my truck as the ultimate "chick magnet."

Life was good.

Funny how an advertisement can change things.

Three years later Nissan mailed me an innocent, attractively designed postcard proclaiming the pending arrival of the completely redesigned 1996 Pathfinder. The picture looked appealing. But I was content with what I had. After all, I loved Big Red.

As you might expect, a national ad campaign featuring this improved edition flooded my TV, the newspapers, and various magazines. Just about everywhere I turned, I saw pictures of the updated Pathfinder.

I'm not sure how or why, but a videotape arrived at my home, promising footage of the fresh features of this redesigned Nissan. Call me curious. I shoved the tape into my VCR. There it was. The shapely lines remained graceful even as the wheels pounded rocks into submission.

GR-R-R-R-R!

The music swelled as the camera angle changed. The view of the soft leather seats and a Bose sound system filled my screen.

Very nice. Very nice indeed.

Admittedly, Nissan's ad strategy was incredibly effective. It sowed the seeds of discontentment in me. Did you know that the majority of advertising works because it makes us *dissatisfied* with what we presently have? In short, advertising works by pushing our "discontentment button."

For the first time in years I started to get picky with my '93. Would you look at that—the silly arm rest is getting worn! What's that noise? A small squeak developed somewhere underneath. A tiny crack appeared in the windshield. I found myself finding fault with my previously unstoppable powerhouse.

In 1998 I couldn't stand it any longer. I made my way to the lion's den—um, dealer showroom—where I betrayed my '93 and leased the latest and greatest. In 1998 I was married and had moved to Nashville, Tennessee, where snow is rarely an issue. Who needed the 4x4 feature? The top-of-the-line 4x2 LE would do. Leather, you bet.

Dark metallic forest-green—sounds dreamy. Matches the sophisticated family image.

Oh, did I mention chrome on the bumpers *and* running boards?

Wouldn't you know, within three days I got stuck in that lousy 4x2. A few wet leaves in the field, and I found myself spinning grass.

As I write, our lease—or should I say "fleece"—is almost up. It's been said that confession is good for the soul. I need to make a confession. Over the past two and a half years at least once *every week* I've wished I had my old Pathfinder back. I'm so mad that I wasn't content with what I had. I could have been driving a perfectly fine vehicle—with no payments.

Contentment. What is it?

How about being satisfied with my present situation? Relaxed? Freed from the need to acquire more of the "stuff" advertisers insist I accumulate? Did you know that the average person in America will watch between 20,000 and 30,000 advertisements on TV each year?

That's a whole lot of discontentment.

Listen to those words again: "I have learned the secret of being content in any and every situation." When the apostle Paul penned this passage, he was sitting in a prison, not sipping Snapple overlooking the Sea of Galilee.

To have contentment isn't to be without aspirations and goals. But when it comes to the acquiring of stuff, be it a large item such as a car or something less extravagant such as adding yet another Beanie Baby to the 107 my daughter already owns, each of us would do well to discover "the secret" of being content, of rejoicing in the blessings God has generously showered upon us. That's why our family has taken the first step toward contentment by hitting the "mute" button whenever the commercials come on.

BUT WAIT, THERE'S MORE!

1. Have you ever watched a TV commercial with the sound off? When your TV fast is over, try it. Count how often the picture changes within those thirty seconds. How much time does the advertiser give us to carefully evaluate each new idea?

2. Read James 4:1-2. What causes the battle within us?

Proper Speech

*But I tell you that men will have to give account on the day
of judgment for every careless word they have spoken.*

MATTHEW 12:36

As decades go, the seventies produced more than their share of
(thankfully) forgotten fads. Bell-bottom pants. Ascots. Day-Glo
Peter Max posters. Black lights. Lime-green shag carpet. Turquoise-
colored kitchen appliances. The Pet Rock. Lava lamps. And the
Wa-Wa guitar pedal.

Another seventies craze was the coffeehouse. These informal gath-
ering places sported homespun music and occasionally a wanna-be
stand-up comic. Hippies sat on folding or beanbag chairs around can-
dle-lit tables, while munching on light snacks and sipping soda pop or
coffee. Those who frequented the coffeehouse scene came primarily to
"chill out" and "groove" to the music. Some came to rap—which had
nothing to do with rap music and everything to do with long, drawn-
out philosophical conversations about the meaning of the cosmos.

I lived in the Philadelphia area during my teen years—that would
be when Richard Nixon was President. On the national scene it was
a turbulent time. The peaceniks battled the "establishment" over U.S.
involvement in the war in Vietnam.

The church meanwhile battled issues such as long hair and so-
called Jesus music. I recall that a number of progressive churches
decided to host a coffeehouse on weekends in their fellowship hall.
A tool to reach the youth. It was a radical strategy—for real.

Thanks to my Christian upbringing, I felt called to engage my
world with the Gospel through music. My friend and fellow guitar-

strumming junior hippie, David Rawlings, and I decided to work up several songs to perform at one of these coffeehouses.

Trust me. This was a big step for any self-conscious teen.

I had complete confidence in my guitar skills. Singing in public, however, was a tad out of my comfort zone.

More like the distance from here to Mars.

Dave picked the songs and arranged the harmonies. I drew up the charts for the guitar parts. We rehearsed for hours. Before school. During lunch. After school. Whenever we could find the time.

The moment of truth came. Our duo was scheduled to be the second act of the evening. I can't recall the day or month. (A therapist might say I'm repressing the memory.) In any case, I remember managing to get sick. My ears were clogged with whatever they get clogged with when you've got a severe head cold.

But the show must go on.

As we launched into our second tune, a Crosby, Stills, Nash & Young favorite, it was clear that my sense of pitch was in jeopardy. To be more precise, my harmony failed to harmonize. I knew it. Who didn't?

From somewhere out in the audience, hiding in the safe harbor of darkness, a stray comment drifted onto stage: "That guy can't sing!"

Ouch!

The rest of the evening was an exercise in torture. To this day I don't have any idea who blurted out such a hurtful comment. But I've got to tell you, I still remember those words as if they were spoken yesterday. That was the last time I sang in public—unless surrounded by the safety of a choir.

How about you? Do you find yourself still replaying the rude, thoughtless words someone spoke to you years ago? Is it any wonder that a loving heavenly Father, the creator of the tongue, would place such a high responsibility on the use of our tongues?

Look again at what Jesus says: You and I must "give account" for "every careless word" we speak. Why? Is this just Jesus' way of offering a divine payback for all the name-calling bullies on the playground? Hardly.

Our Lord places a premium on proper speech because He understands that "Reckless words pierce like a sword, but the tongue of the wise brings healing" (Prov. 12:18). In other words, our words can lift or crush the human spirit. They can breathe life and healing or foster sickness and death.

I know. I've been wounded by such words.

I know. I've spoken such words.

I know. By God's grace, I will be more careful about how I speak from this day on.

BUT WAIT, THERE'S MORE!

1. The overwhelming majority of TV comedians today rely upon a routine heavily peppered with profanity. Read Ephesians 5:4 and see what the Scriptures say about such coarse joking.

2. Is it wise to view television programs where harsh, disrespectful, even mean-spirited words are tossed around with no regard for the damage they do? How might I be influenced as I listen to such damaging patterns of speech?

Galactic Implications

When I consider your heavens, the work of your fingers,
the moon and the stars, which you have set in place,
what is man that you are mindful of him,
the son of man that you care for him?

PSALM 8:3–4

During the month of October 1997, something so unbelievable happened in outer space that it literally rocked the universe. Can you remember what this extraordinary event was? Frankly, I'd be surprised if many even heard about it. It barely made the evening news. I'm referring to the awesome collision of two entire galaxies.

Were we really that busy watching *Wheel of Fortune* to have missed something so staggering? Sad to say, few of us Earthlings took notice of this eruption in our galactic neighborhood.

Let me put this event into perspective. The Earth rotates within the Milky Way galaxy along with Mars, Jupiter, Pluto, and the other planets. Imagine, if you can, all of the planets, stars, moons, and other celestial bodies in our galaxy slamming into another galaxy of similar size. That would be news, wouldn't it? Why didn't the media give such a remarkable phenomenon the coverage it deserves?

Are they perhaps uncomfortable with the implications?

Must be.

Especially when you realize that this breathtaking smashup was actually photographed in living color by the Hubble space telescope. I've seen the pictures, and they're more dramatic than any car chase or explosion Hollywood's collective fertile minds could manufacture.

Think about it. If CNN, *USA Today*, and the other major news organizations attempted to cover a story of this magnitude with any real substance, they'd have to explore difficult questions such as the "God factor." Presumably, that's something the media elite are uncomfortable tackling.

I, for one, came away with several questions of my own.

What caused the celestial smashup?

Are we next?

If so, how do you stop it?!

The implications of this event eclipse the scope of our puny human capabilities. I know I was prompted to ask: "How big is my God?" After all, light travels at 186,000 miles per second. At that pace light will travel 5.6 trillion miles in just one year (also known as one light year).

So when light travels 5.6 trillion miles in one year, that's really far! If your mind hasn't started to overload yet, here's what blew *my* circuits. The location of this galactic crash was *63 million light years* away (that's 63,000,000 x 5.6 trillion). WOW!

I'm thankful the Hubble space telescope captured the dramatic encounter in all of its magnificent detail, because it enables us to have a fresh perspective on the greatness and power of God. As amazing as this event is, you may be wondering what does it have to do with television. Read on.

Meet Heather. This fifteen-year-old teenager sent me the following emotionally charged letter taking issue with my perspective on television and music choices. She writes from Madison, Wisconsin:

Dear Bob,

You never fail to anger me with your demented point of view. It's comments [on entertainment] like that that make me wonder just how thick your skull really is! Also, the type of lifestyle that you are urging (or should I say brainwashing) your readers to lead is a totally sheltered, unreal, impossible, not to mention BORING way of life. Why don't you just lighten up and realize that almost no one's life is devoted entirely to God.

One thing I've always appreciated about teenagers is that you rarely have to ask, "So tell me, how do you *really* feel? You know, could you be a little more specific?"

It was Heather's final observation (that "almost no one's life is devoted entirely to God") that got to me. Essentially, her justification for making poor entertainment choices boiled down to a dwarfed view of God.

You see, when it comes to developing a world-life view, especially as it pertains to the arena of the arts and entertainment, *it is our view of God* that is the heart of the matter. The smaller my view of God, His power and His majesty, the more likely I am to tolerate, yes, even enjoy art that is morally offensive to Him.

By contrast, when I find myself standing in awe of the magnitude of God's power—including His handiwork in space—the less I'm tempted to break His heart. Instead, I find myself desiring to please Him with my whole being—every thought, word, and deed. Now I ask myself: "Are a few fleeting moments of amusement worth grieving the God of the galaxies?"

Some years ago J. B. Phillips wrote a popular book whose title and theme was *Your God Is Too Small*.

How big is your God?

BUT WAIT, THERE'S MORE!

1. Go outdoors one night this week and search the sky with eyes of wonderment. Then consider answering the question the psalmist raised in Psalm 8:4.

2. If you have a computer, check out the pictures of this celestial collision (http://oposite.stsci.edu/pubinfo/pr/97/34/).

3. When you rent a video or view a TV show, consider whether or not your selection will bring sadness to the heart of your heavenly Father. How might you honor with your choices the one who sustains the galaxies in the palm of His hand?

A Matter of Time

Show me, O LORD, my life's end and the number of my days;
let me know how fleeting is my life.

PSALM 39:4

Take a minute right now to count how many clocks, watches, or other timepieces you have around the house. Go ahead, I'll wait. Take as much time as you need. As you count, don't forget appliances such as your microwave, oven, computer, VCR, and telephone answering machine, all of which usually have a built-in clock. (By the way, prior to 1687 clocks had just one hand—the hour hand.)

How many did you find?

In our house I counted twenty-one different devices—including the clocks in our two cars. No wonder I'm so exhausted whenever Daylight Savings Time comes and goes, requiring me to change all of those clocks either forward or backward an hour!

Did you ever consider why life requires the use of so many clocks? Evidently, our society puts a high price tag on time. As the saying goes, "Time is money."

My brother Steve was a missionary living in Uganda for several years. One of the first things he did upon arriving in that beautiful African country was to toss out his watch. He told me that their culture wasn't obsessed with time the way American culture is.

Now take a few moments to list as many different commonly used expressions that incorporate the words *time, second,* or *minute.* Feel free to include extensions of those words, too, such as *timing.* You might want to make your list before reading ahead to my list.

Here's what I came up with: "What time is it?" "Time will tell,"

"Just a minute, please," "I'll be there in a second," "Turn back the hands of time," "moment in time," "Check the timetable," "What perfect timing," "Give him the time of day," "I'm counting the seconds," "He called a time out," "I'll check my Day-Timer," "Please be on time," "That's the last time," "Time's up," "Time is of the essence," and "What a time-saver."

Just for fun, can you think of a few songs that use time as a metaphor? ("Time in a Bottle" and "Time After Time.") It's clear that time is a big issue for us.

With that in mind, here's one last question. How much time will the average American—you and I—spend watching TV by the time we reach retirement at age sixty-five? Let's run the numbers. It's a documented fact that most people spend three hours *per day* viewing various television programs.

Watch what happens when we do the math:

```
    3    national average number of hours per day watching TV
  x 7    days per week
 = 21    hours of TV per week


   21    hours per week
 x 50    weeks per year (assuming you don't watch on vacation)
= 1,050  total hours spent watching TV per year
```

We learned in an earlier chapter that various medical associations such as the American Academy of Pediatrics strongly recommend that children refrain from all TV-viewing until they reach age two, and then that they see only an hour per day until at least age five. These professionals are concerned that the tube has a negative effect on early childhood development. For the sake of the argument, let's assume that we don't permit TV-viewing until age five.

Now watch what happens:

```
  1,050   hours per year
   x 60   years of TV-viewing (from age five to sixty-five)
= 63,000  total hours spent staring at the box
```

Hard to believe, isn't it? If you and I aren't careful, we'll log 63,000 hours sitting in a chair while our body atrophies before television's hypnotic electronic eye. And that's just at the national average. There are millions of people who view more than three hours a day! Of course, my mathematical mind wants to quantify this figure into something more meaningful:

63,000 cumulative hours of TV by age sixty-five
÷ 8,760 total number of hours in one year (24 hours/day x 365/year)
= 7.19 number of years *viewing* TV

The first time I did this calculation the thought crossed my mind, *Boy, I could go to college two more times instead of vegging in front of the tube! Certainly I could at least get a master's degree.*

Or spend more intimate time with my children.

Or plan dozens of special things to do with my wife.

I wonder what King David would have said about the idea of wasting away seven precious years of life in such a useless activity. In a way David did comment: "Show me, O LORD, my life's end and the number of my days; let me know how fleeting is my life." He knew that there's no stopping time. It's over before we know it.

Time spent is time gone.

Forever.

Time is so precious, so valuable, that you and I can't buy more at any price. The next time you see one of those many clocks throughout your house, why not reflect on these inspired words of the psalmist. Speaking of time, can you believe you've just completed your first full week without television? Congratulations! Keep up the good work!

BUT WAIT, THERE'S MORE!

1. Even if everything on TV were praiseworthy, what else might you do with seven years of your life besides watching the TV?

2. Remember the saying, "Time is money"? Evaluate your return

on this investment of your time. What dividends does TV watching pay you?

3. I don't mean to over-spiritualize matters. But imagine the positive impact on your relationship to the Lord if instead of consuming seven years of television, you spent a portion of that time reading your Bible and praying.

A Bridge of Friendship

*Therefore go and make disciples of all nations, baptizing them
in the name of the Father and of the Son and of the Holy Spirit,
and teaching them to obey everything I have commanded you.*

MATTHEW 28:19-20A

The other day my wife and I sat down to watch an awards program
on CBS. Trust me, that in and of itself is almost a miracle. I detest the
smug, self-congratulatory attitude of these programs. However, this
particular evening I tried to have an open mind.

It wasn't more than a few moments before the various presenters and recipients began to pepper their comments with profanity. As
they tossed around vulgar words without a blush, our living room
was invaded by language we don't permit—nor choose to use—in the
DeMoss home.

Thanks for nothing, CBS.

We turned off the set—again.

This isn't the first time prime time has behaved more like "prime
slime." In fact, more often than not, the television remains off in our
home. You see, we have this pesky family policy: "The TV isn't
allowed to say or display things *we* shouldn't say or display."

As my wife and I sat in the silence that evening, I thought back
to a related experience. I had taken my then eleven-year-old daughter on a "daddy-daughter date." That particular night we had dinner
and a movie. The G-rated picture would have been a special treat had
it not been for the promotional teasers packed with violence and
unacceptable language shown before the film. I'm sure you've had
similar experiences.

So what gives?

Why do today's movies and television programs have to be so hostile to the family? Is there any hope that Hollywood will ever have a change of heart and one day use their international platform to create films and TV shows that elevate the human spirit rather than degrade it?

An even more important question might be, "What's the best way for you and me to impact and change the direction of Hollywood?"

Boycotts?

Massive letter-writing campaigns?

Strong-arm tactics on advertisers?

Although there may be some merit in these approaches, Dr. Larry Poland, president of Mastermedia International, Inc., has a different idea: *Pray* for those who create and promote the media we consume.

Dr. Poland founded Mastermedia with a dual purpose—to encourage those who are believers inside the Hollywood establishment and to evangelize the lost therein. He reflects, "After more than a decade of meeting and working with these key professionals, I can tell you that many of them seek personal peace, love, forgiveness, and spiritual power."

They do? Who would have guessed?

Dr. Poland was also surprised to learn that this is a wide-open mission field. Virtually *no other* Christian ministry has attempted to nurture relationships with these influential leaders. He describes his approach as building "a bridge of friendship" through face-to-face contact, as a vehicle to share Christ with them. Along the way he's made several discoveries.

For instance, more than 60 percent of middle management in Hollywood are Jewish. That percentage increases the higher up the corporate ladder you go. He also learned that there are, surprisingly, small pockets of believers who meet for prayer and Bible study on a regular basis at several of the major studios.

When I spoke with Dr. Poland about his vision, he said, "Bob, if you desire a change in what Hollywood produces, begin by changing hearts." He added, "I remember one executive who got saved and who called me several months later to explain that he's using a lot more 'red ink' on scripts. He found himself crossing out objectionable scenes, language, and humor. Why? Because God was at work in his heart!"

Jesus said to go into "all the world." Wouldn't that include the land occupied by those who create the television we consume? Indeed, Hollywood *can* be transformed—one heart at a time.

BUT WAIT, THERE'S MORE!

1. Why is so little being done to evangelize executives in the film and television industries? Would you consider becoming a "missionary" to Hollywood?

2. How might today's entertainment change if some of the key leaders were to come to Christ?

3. Take a minute right now to pray for Larry Poland's ministry. Why not add him to your regular prayer list?

Making Memories

Finally, brothers, whatever is true, whatever is noble,
whatever is right, whatever is pure, whatever is lovely,
whatever is admirable—if anything is excellent or praiseworthy—
think about such things.

PHILIPPIANS 4:8

When Uncle Butch told me he put snakes under my bed, I believed him. As he turned to leave my bedroom, he smirked and then switched off the light for good measure. Lying alone in the dark, I could picture those scaly, legless serpents licking their chops. I knew they were waiting for me to stick my foot over the edge so they could inject their venom into my big toe.

I was five years old at the time.

I still possess a rather active imagination.

Funny—to this day I have a healthy fear of snakes.

Is there a connection? Maybe.

How about you? What prompts your heart to panic—and why? Further, could there be a relationship between something you've watched on television or viewed at a movie and how you react in certain situations?

Actually, it's highly probable. At least that's the finding of a study from the University of Michigan. Researchers Kristen Harrison, Ph.D., and Joanne Cantor, Ph.D., have conclusively documented a relationship between early childhood exposure to "fright stimuli" and a prolonged reoccurrence of fear associated with the original exposure.

In fact, 90 percent of those participating in their study experienced a lasting impact from scary films and other frightening entertainment viewed as young persons. Harrison and Cantor detailed their findings in a fascinating report entitled, "Tales from the Screen: Enduring Fright Reactions to Scary Media."

The researchers studied a sample of college students (average age, twenty) from the University of Michigan and the University of Wisconsin-Madison. The range of symptoms reported by these participants to the memory of the frightening stimuli included crying or screaming (26 percent), trembling or shaking (24 percent), nausea or stomach pain (20 percent); and clinging to a companion and experiencing an increased heart rate were both experienced by 18 percent. Many indicated they had experienced chills, fever, dizziness, and feelings of paralysis.

Okay, but what does all of this mean?

Let's say you watched *Jaws* as a six-year-old. According to this report, as many as fourteen years later you would be a prime candidate for an increased level of anxiety and fear of stepping foot into the ocean—due to exposure to that film. Perhaps it was a film about airplane crashes. If you viewed that as a child, chances are good that you'd have a heightened level of fearfulness at the suggestion of taking a trip by plane.

These researchers found several other key facts. For instance, the younger the participant was at the time of the original exposure to "fright media," the more likely the person would report lasting implications.

And when asked where these participants had their first exposure, more than 30 percent replied with theater, 30 percent said home video, 21 percent pointed to broadcast television, and about 15 percent listed cable.

Look at it this way. If someone had lovingly prevented these children (who are now college-aged students) from being exposed to the frightening scene at the theater, on TV, or in a video rental, these students would have been spared years of unnecessary anxiety.

Choices have consequences.

Likewise, if I as a parent choose to look the other way and permit my children to view whatever they like, I may be sentencing them to a lifelong struggle with preventable fear syndromes. Is it any wonder that the apostle Paul encourages us to think on "whatever is pure, whatever is lovely, whatever is admirable"?

As I've said elsewhere, "the things that play in the theater of our mind shape the habits of our heart."

What's playing in your theater?

How might that be shaping your heart?

BUT WAIT, THERE'S MORE!

1. The researchers didn't conclude how long a person's enduring fright reaction could potentially last. Some had already wrestled with their fears for fourteen years. It's possible that fear may stalk them their entire lifetime.

2. But there's hope! Read Psalm 34:4 and Revelation 21:4-5a. God can deliver us from our fears, and He promises to one day erase all of our fears, remove all of our pain, and wipe away all of our tears. Even so, wouldn't it be wise to avoid filling our mind with these images in the first place?

Fear Not Failure

They were all trying to frighten us, thinking,
"Their hands will get too weak for the work, and it will not
be completed." But I prayed, "Now strengthen my hands."

NEHEMIAH 6:9

I'll never forget the summer when time stood still. It was 1970, and against seemingly impossible odds, our Little League team actually made the playoffs. By the fifth inning it was clear we were being stomped by the other team. Crushed is closer to the truth.

We were down eleven to three.

Our opponents were taller, stronger, faster. Invincible.

"Never say die," the coach advised as we took the bench preparing for our turn in the bottom of the fifth. I'm not sure if it was his pep talk or the Gatorade, but somehow we managed to load the bases—with two outs.

That's when I headed for the plate, my trusty thirty-two-inch black-and-white bat in hand. I was the "clean-up" hitter.

At the moment "washed-up" was how I felt.

I hadn't had a hit all day.

I kicked the dust in the batter's box—just like the pros did on TV—and then turned to face the pitcher. His evil eye glared at me as if to say, "You wimp. You'll never touch it." Their catcher read his signal and started on me with, "You ain't no batter, son."

The pitch was a high and outside fastball.

Whoosh!

I swear a guy's toupee in the third row blew back from the wind caused by my swing-and-a-miss.

"My mom could have hit that with her eyes closed." Mr. Catcher provided his commentary.

Another pitch. Another swing. Another strike. The countdown to failure was now "no balls, two strikes."

That's when time stood still.

I thought everyone could hear my heart pounding inside my chest. The visitors jeered. The home fans cheered. The bases were loaded. I was one strike away from failure. Oddly, I remembered that Babe Ruth—who back then held the world lifetime record for home runs—also held the record for most strikeouts, a whopping 1,316. That provided little comfort.

His next pitch flamed toward the plate. This time the crack of my bat sent the ball to deep right field.

Very deep.

I had hit my first grand slam! The momentum created by those runs propelled us to win the game and ultimately the championship.

What's that story got to do with the TV turnoff? Plenty. You and your family are ten days into this unique challenge. And it's my guess you've had "friends" or even family members—not to mention the devil—who have attempted to dissuade you from pressing on.

I can hear the naysayers now: "No TV? Why do such a crazy thing?" "What's the point? TV is here to stay. Besides, think of what you're missing." "Do you sincerely think this will change the TV industry? Ha!" "Besides, nobody can go a whole month without television."

Just as the opposition attempted to discourage me with their verbal jabs during that Little League game, you may be faced with folks sitting on the sidelines of life who mock your efforts to try something new. Something radical. Something real. Something God placed upon your heart.

The Old Testament prophet Nehemiah endured such ridicule. The Lord placed in Nehemiah's heart a desire to rebuild the wall, which had been reduced to rubble, around Jerusalem. When the surrounding nations learned Nehemiah and the Jews had undertaken such an ambitious goal, they tried to "frighten us," Nehemiah explains. "When Sanballat heard that we were rebuilding the wall . . . he ridiculed the Jews" (Nehemiah 4:1).

The taunting turned mean: "What they are building—if even a fox climbed up on it, he would break down their wall of stones!" (v. 3). But Nehemiah refused to listen to those who pressured the Jews to forsake their goal. Eventually, Nehemiah reports, "We rebuilt the wall till all of it reached half its height, for the people worked with all their heart" (v. 6).

When Sanballat and company saw the progress, they planned to attack the Jews as a last-ditch effort to stop them. It's at this point that Nehemiah prayed, "Now strengthen my hands."

How is your family doing on your TV fast?

Do you feel like quitting?

Are friends laughing at your "little experiment"?

Then do as Nehemiah did. Ask the Lord to strengthen your hands. To fortify your desire to discover the benefits of life without dependence on the TV. While you're at it, pray for a gracious attitude when you respond to those who don't share your passion.

Hang in there! I know you can go the distance.

I've got the bat to prove it.

BUT WAIT, THERE'S MORE!

1. It's been reported that Thomas Edison, the father of numerous inventions, tried upwards of 50,000 different experiments before perfecting the storage battery. When asked if he ever thought of giving up along the way since so many experiments resulted in nothing, Edison reflected, "Results? Why, I know 50,000 things that won't work!"

2. What answer might you offer someone who thinks you should quit before finishing the TV fast?

3. Read and discuss Galatians 6:9: "Let us not become weary in doing good, for at the proper time we will reap a harvest if we do not give up."

When You Haven't Got a Prayer

The prayer of a righteous man
is powerful and effective.

JAMES 5:16B

I remember the first time I visited a church where my best friend in high school attended. Before we arrived, he warned me, "Bob, this is a highly liturgical church." Huh? "Well," he explained, "we read prayers from a prayer book and use formal rituals in our worship service."

Initially, the thought of prewritten prayers was, well, stifling. Shouldn't prayer be spontaneous? You know, fresh and from the heart?

Admittedly, I was pleasantly surprised with the experience. I came to see that there can be a real beauty when prior thought is given to the preparation of a prayer, especially when words fail us in unique situations.

That's why today I'd like to provide a number of specific prayers to help you get started praying for the Lord's help in your entertainment choices.

In fact, let's engage your entire family while we're at it. You may want to move to a comfortable work space such as a desk or the kitchen table. Locate seven 4-x-6 index cards and a fine-point marker. Below I've provided seven Scriptures and prayerful insights relating to various aspects of the world of entertainment. In just a minute either type, hand-write, or photocopy that information onto the index cards.

On the top line write the subject heading I've proposed. Next copy the Scripture reference on the first few lines of the card. Below that write out the prayer reflection. Feel free to copy these verbatim, or rewrite them in your own words. Tonight at dinner have someone draw one card to read either before or after the meal.

It's so simple and yet so powerful.

Ready? Let's get started.

TELEVISION

"But I tell you that men will have to give account on the day of judgment for every careless word they have spoken. For by your words you will be acquitted, and by your words you will be condemned." (MATTHEW 12:36-37)

Prayer Reflection: Dear Jesus, the television can have such a strong influence on our family. In the Scriptures it's clear You place a premium on proper speech. When I sit down to watch the TV, help me to have the strength to turn off a program where improper language is spoken. Amen.

MOVIES

"Finally, brothers, whatever is true, whatever is noble, whatever is right, whatever is pure, whatever is lovely, whatever is admirable—if anything is excellent or praiseworthy—think about such things." (PHILIPPIANS 4:8)

Prayer Reflection: Dear Jesus, thank You for the gift of imagination. But there are so many temptations to let my imagination stray. Help me to seek out only the praiseworthy options at the theater, even if I'm with my friends or at a slumber party. Amen.

VIDEOS

"So God said to Noah, 'I am going to put an end to all people, for the earth is filled with violence because of them. I am surely going to destroy both them and the earth.'" (GENESIS 6:13)

Prayer Reflection: Dear Jesus, in the days of Noah You were so angry with all of the violence in the world that You sent the Flood. Today I know the violence in videos makes You sad. So help us to find selections that don't celebrate the use of violence. Amen.

TELEVISION

"If we confess our sins, He is faithful and righteous to forgive us our sins and to cleanse us from all unrighteousness." (1 JOHN 1:9 NASB)

Prayer Reflection: Dear Jesus, I confess that it's not easy to always please You with the viewing choices I make. Forgive me when I get lazy, tired, or don't care enough to do what's right. Amen.

MOVIES

"Put to death, therefore, whatever belongs to your earthly nature: sexual immorality, impurity, lust, evil desires and greed, which is idolatry. Because of these, the wrath of God is coming." (COLOSSIANS 3:5-6)

Prayer Reflection: Dear Jesus, it's fun to go to the movies. But when I watch a film or rent a video, help me to compare what I'm seeing to this list of sinful behaviors. If what I'm viewing displeases You, give me the courage to leave or turn it off. Amen.

TELEVISION

"Let us fix our eyes on Jesus, the author and perfecter of our faith, who for the joy set before him endured the cross, scorning its shame, and sat down at the right hand of the throne of God." (HEBREWS 12:2)

Prayer Reflection: Dear Jesus, sometimes kids at school mock me because I'm not allowed to watch certain shows or channels such as MTV. But when the world mocked You, You resisted. Help me to have that same strength and courage to do the right thing. Amen.

VIDEOS

"I will praise the LORD all my life; I will sing praise to my God as long as I live." (PSALM 146:2)

Prayer Reflection: Dear Jesus, thank You for inspiring Christians to make music videos for me to enjoy. They really help me to grow in my faith. Help me to find good contemporary Christian alternatives to build a strong video collection. Amen.

By the way, after you've exhausted your supply of cards, why not invite the family to come up with another seven!

BUT WAIT, THERE'S MORE!

1. What might Satan do to discourage your commitment to a more focused life of prayer—especially in the area of personal entertainment choices?

2. As you incorporate these prayer cards into your family routine, consider also memorizing this simple petition: "Lord, help me to love what You love and hate what You hate."

Too Close to the Flame

Then she called, "Samson, the Philistines are upon you!"
He awoke from his sleep and thought, "I'll go out as before and
shake myself free." But he did not know that the LORD had left him.

JUDGES 16:20

The ABC television network struck gold in 1999 with the debut of a new quiz show called *Who Wants to Be a Millionaire?* A contestant must answer a series of fifteen questions, each more difficult than the previous one. The millionaire-wanna-be must choose between four multiple-choice answers. If he or she answers correctly, the jackpot increases. At any point a contestant can take the earnings or try for the big win—and risk losing a huge portion of what has already been won.

I doubt that ABC would use it, but I believe I've discovered the perfect million-dollar question: "How many births in the Bible were foretold by an angel?" One? Three? Five? Twelve?

Three?

Is that your final answer?

The correct response is five: Ishmael, Isaac, Samson, John the Baptist, and Jesus.

Samson? What's he doing on the celestial announcement list?

I did some digging and discovered that there are numerous similarities between Samson's life and that of John the Baptist. Both were born to mothers who were barren. Both arrived during a time when Israel was occupied by a foreign power. The Philistines had dominated Israel for forty years when Samson was born; the Romans were in control during John's birth.

Both were born to be Nazirites—that is, dedicated to the high calling of the Lord's work. And both men were destined to serve as prophetic voices pointing the way to freedom.

But that's where the comparison screeches to a halt. Unlike John the Baptist, Samson had a weakness for women. In Judges 14 Samson ignored the wishes of his parents that he marry an Israelite, and he sought a wife from the enemy instead. In chapter 16 we learn that Samson spent the night with a prostitute. His next and final exploit was a Philistine woman named Delilah.

You probably know the rest of the story. Delilah begs Samson day by day to tell her the source of his superhuman strength. After a string of bogus answers, he finally confides in this woman who, by the way, was attempting to kill him. Samson explained, "No razor has ever been used on my head . . . because I have been a Nazirite set apart to God since birth. If my head were shaved, my strength would leave me, and I would become as weak as any other man" (Judges 16:17).

With that confession, Samson fell asleep on the lap of Delilah. She, in turn, shaved off his hair and called for the Philistine thugs to attack him.

Some girlfriend, eh?

How did Samson respond? He thought, *I'll go out as before and shake myself free.* The Scripture then adds this painful insight: "But he did not know that the LORD had left him." Samson was powerless to do anything while his eyes were gouged out by his sworn enemies.

A couple of important questions come to mind. What was the judge of Israel doing sleeping with the enemy? When did Samson lose sight of his spiritual calling? Did it happen all at once—or over time through a series of personal compromises? Didn't he know he was flirting with fire?

There's an important lesson for you and me in this story. If Samson, whose birth was proclaimed by an angel of God, who had extraordinary strength, and who was fully aware of the Lord's claim on his life, can be seduced, what about us lightweight twenty-first-century believers who bask in the lap of television's guiding light far too often?

Can we really play "footsies" with the Delilah of the entertain-

ment culture and remain unaffected? Have we become too comfortable and too casual with the very thing that has the ability to blur our
spiritual vision? Is it possible that we, like Samson, could compromise our choices so often that we wouldn't realize we had grieved the
Holy Spirit of God (Eph. 4:30) and that, like Samson, the Lord's presence had been withdrawn?

Don't get me wrong. There are good options on TV. However,
those selections are few and far between. Which is why the time you
and I are spending away from the television is the perfect time to get
refocused, to renew our vows with our First Love.

BUT WAIT, THERE'S MORE!

1. Have you ever thought, *I know what I believe. I'm not worried. I can
   watch anything on TV, and it won't affect me?* In light of the story of
   Samson, how might you rethink that position?

2. First Corinthians 10:12 provides this word of caution to all believers: "So, if you think you are standing firm, be careful that you
   don't fall!" Discuss the implications for future TV consumption.

Backstage Bloopers

*May the words of my mouth and the meditation of my heart
be pleasing in your sight, O LORD, my Rock and my Redeemer.*

PSALM 19:14

I saw *Phantom of the Opera* at the Ahmanson Theater in Los Angeles.
What an unforgettable experience. Millions of dollars were spent to
properly outfit that auditorium for what is simply an incredible production. No wonder *Phantom* sold out virtually every night—for several years.

This night was especially enchanting as my date and I got a rare
personal tour of the behind-the-scenes action. We started in the
wardrobe room where numerous gowns, some valued at $25,000
apiece, hung safely in place. I had to touch one just to say I did.

Our guide steered us below the surface of the stage through a
maze of dimly lit secret passageways. He pointed out dozens of trap-
doors used for actor entrances and exits during the opera. He walked
us into the orchestra pit—a tight space ten feet beneath the auditorium where the conductor and musicians set the mood each evening.
And everywhere we walked, miles of various audio cables snaked
their way underneath the stage.

No wonder tickets were $75 apiece.

As the saying goes, there's more than meets the eye.

In some ways, I wasn't completely surprised at what we witnessed backstage. Over the years I've had my share of on-stage per-
formances. I've conducted my Learn to Discern seminar in
hundreds of cities across North America. Several have been hosted
on "famous stages," including where Jim Morrison (of the Doors

fame) had performed. In Memphis I spoke from a stage where Elvis had shaken his pelvis.

Then there was the night in Edmonton, Alberta, Canada, where an elderly man approached me backstage with a special request before we began: "Bob, I'm hard of hearing. Would you mind wearing this?" He held out a small lapel microphone and transmitter. "This transmits directly into my hearing aid," he explained, adding, "I don't want to miss anything you say."

A reasonable request.

After all, as a public speaker I'm accustomed to wearing a wireless lapel mike tied into the public address system. I agreed and clipped his mike onto my jacket next to mine.

There was, however, one key difference. The mike I normally use was equipped with a special "mute" button in case I coughed. And the mute feature prevented the audience from hearing my backstage conversations with the production team. It was only after this man left that I noticed his microphone didn't have a mute option.

Oh, great!

Now *everything* I said for the next two hours would be heard by this stranger! My first reaction was, *I've got to be on my best behavior. There's no room for bloopers tonight!*

How about you?

Imagine you agreed to wear a microphone that captured and transmitted your every word, joke, or comment into someone's hearing aid. How might you temper your words, knowing that "someone's listening" each time you open your mouth?

Let's take that idea one step further. What if *every thought* you had was transmitted? Revealed. Exposed.

Kind of scary, huh?

That's precisely what King David was doing when he invited the Lord to be pleased with both "the words of my mouth and the meditation of my heart." In reality God already knows every word we speak (see Psalm 139:4). He knows our thoughts. All of them. Those dark, secret places where no "mute" button can ever conceal what's playing inside our hearts.

Why would David ever volunteer for such intense scrutiny? Because he longed to live his life as a "pleasing" sacrifice of obedience to his Redeemer. Social critic Os Guinness said it best: "Live your life before the audience of One."

BUT WAIT, THERE'S MORE!

1. In Psalm 39:1 David said, "I will watch my ways and keep my tongue from sin; I will put a muzzle on my mouth." Can you think of a television program that would benefit from David's muzzle?

2. In 2 Corinthians 10:5b the apostle Paul says, "We take captive every thought to make it obedient to Christ." Does indiscriminate TV-viewing work against this goal? How?

Food for Thought

Therefore you shall lay up these words of mine in your heart
and in your soul, and bind them as a sign on your hand,
and they shall be as frontlets between your eyes.
You shall teach them to your children, speaking of them
when you sit in your house, when you walk by the way,
when you lie down, and when you rise up.

DEUTERONOMY 11:18-19 NKJV

Here's a fun food fact you'll probably never use: Americans eat enough hot dogs each year that, if linked end to end, they'd reach the moon and back!

Speaking of food, according to the National Restaurant Association, Americans were projected to spend a record $376 *billion* eating at restaurants during the year 2000. Let me put that into perspective. Americans spend more on eating out than the value of the entire gross national product of countries such as Denmark, Norway, and Sweden.[2]

Frankly, I'm old enough to remember when the first "fast-food" joint opened in our town back in the mid-sixties.

I was ten years old, and gas was a mere twenty-seven cents a gallon.

Rotary dial phones worked just fine.

And only the "rich" dined at restaurants.

As a child, I recall that we simply did not eat out except on rare occasions. Mom's cooking was superior and, well, expected. Besides, eating at home was less costly, specially with five children devouring dinner.

What about a special Sunday meal after church? For us the question was never "Where shall we go?" but "Who will prepare it?" Dad or Mom? (Mom usually won that vote!)

Today with more than $1 billion spent every day at local eateries, the tables have been turned. It's the rare occasion when families join hands around the dining table for a home-cooked meal.

Here in Nashville creative restaurateurs, recognizing this void in American family life, have attempted to recapture the good ol' days by advertising their "family-style" Sunday lunch. Rather than offering individual meals from a menu, the restaurant provides one family meal served on big plates piled high with food, which are passed around to create a sense of family unity.

How nice.

But more often than not, we "grab" fast food on the go. The yummy smell of a hot breakfast wafting through the house doesn't greet hungry children before school. Who has time or energy to cook, especially at that hour? Just hit the drive-through.

Lunch? Let 'em buy it at the school cafeteria.

Dinner? "Um, where would you like to go tonight, dear? Burger Bash? The Freaky Fajita? Chicken Lickin'?" Worse, in many homes all must fend for themselves.

Don't get me wrong. My family has experienced its share of sniffing drive-through exhaust while awaiting our sack of sustenance. And we enjoy going out for lunch after church. But deep down I think that we believers have lost something special. Indeed, we've misplaced something of paramount importance to the well-being of our homes—and to our faith.

Faith? What's that got to do with *where* we eat?

Take a moment to reread today's passage. Notice that Moses encouraged the Israelites to "teach [God's words] to your children." His idea was to make the exchange a natural, ongoing dialogue that would take place as we sit at home and walk along the road. In fact, this conversation about the Lord was to be part of the fabric of daily life, from "when you lie down" to "when you rise up."

Admittedly, our daily lives are so busy that the times in a day when the whole family comes together are rare.

We don't take walks together.

We don't work together.

About the only event left that brings us in proximity with one another—aside from watching TV—is the evening meal. But, as I've noted, in recent years even this has been lost due to eating out or family members going in different directions.

As I think back to my childhood, dinner was the time to safely share our hearts within the privacy of our cozy dining room. Each night Dad would read Scripture, and we kids would ask questions or make an observation perhaps based on something that had happened that day at school. As we got older, each of us took turns leading the evening devotion.

The idea of daily devotions after dinner is one tradition my wife and I are working on to nurture our household. That is yet another good reason to keep the TV off during meals.

How about your home? Why not start a new dinner devotional habit this month?

Speaking of new habits, guess what? You're well on your way with two TV-free weeks under your belt. Way to go! I knew you could do it. Press on!

BUT WAIT, THERE'S MORE!

1. A study in 1999 by the National Center on Addiction and Substance Abuse at Columbia University discovered that teenagers who typically don't eat their dinner with the family have a substance abuse rate 2.5 times higher than teenagers who eat dinner each night with their families.[3] Why do you think this is so?

2. Are you ever embarrassed to pray out loud or hold hands as a family at a restaurant? Does this dynamic of eating in a public place hamper your family's prayer life?

3. When was the last time you saw a family eating out engaged in family devotions after the meal?

Treasure Island

For where your treasure is, there your heart will be also.

MATTHEW 6:21 NKJV

How would you best describe Ann Landers?

The advice lady?

The sage of our age?

The queen of common sense?

The *World Almanac* describes her as the "most influential woman" in the United States. Why? If the *Guinness Book of World Records* is accurate, she's the most widely syndicated columnist anywhere on the planet. And my guess is that she has more honorary degrees from various colleges and universities than any other pundit—thirty-two and counting.

Is it any wonder that millions of readers catch her daily column, which she's penned faithfully for more than forty years? Readers love her wit and wisdom, her charm and her "uncommon good sense." What's more, they trust her.

Speaking of trust, the liner notes for her book *Wake Up and Smell the Coffee* proclaim, "Whatever the issue, she always says the right thing."

Always?

That's a tall order.

With all due respect, Ann Landers dealt a real doozy in her advice to a woman called "Couch Potato's Wife in Arizona." This poor housewife was ready to punt her husband out of the marriage because of his addiction to watching sports on TV.

Ms. Potato explained, "It's bad enough in the summer with baseball games, but when football season starts, I become completely invisible." Not happy about her spot on the sidelines, she fumed: "In the past several years, he's become a rabid basketball fan, so now he is obsessed 365 days a year."

Her difficulties with this TV-obsessed husband can be traced to the beginning. She explains, "I knew I was in trouble on our honeymoon. While sunbathing on a beach in beautiful Puerto Vallarta, Mexico, my husband said, 'Enough of this. Let's go back to the hotel room.' I was delighted, thinking he had romance in mind."

Are you sitting down, sports fans?

"The truth was, he wanted to watch the NBA finals."

She went on to describe how she's attempted to involve him in any mutual real-life activity, but alas to no avail. Like a trooper, she even tried sitting with him while he sat glued to the tube, but "the games have no meaning for me, and I don't enjoy them."

Out of ideas, energy, and patience, she told Ann Landers, "If he changes the channel 'just to see the score' one more time while I'm watching my favorite TV show, I may call a lawyer."

What would your advice be to this dear soul?

Here's what the most influential woman in the United States suggested: "Pay a visit to a store that sells TVs. Buy yourself a table model and save your marriage."[4]

Excuse me?

Save your marriage by buying another television? Brilliant. Why didn't I think of that?

Sorry, Ann, but that's about as helpful as purchasing a second refrigerator if your spouse has an eating disorder. This man has a severe problem prioritizing the truly important things in his life. He prized the mass consumption of TV sports above all other commitments—some of which he swore before God to do (include cherishing, loving, and honoring his wife). And that's wrong.

Very wrong.

No way should his wife become an accomplice to this addiction.

I realize this situation presents an extreme picture of TV usage. At the same time, there's an important lesson in it for you and me.

Listen again to the words of Jesus, "Where your treasure is, there your heart will be also."

The context of Christ's admonishment was the need for people to become rich toward God. To seek first the kingdom and its righteousness. To invest in things that have eternal value, such as discipleship, evangelism, worship, praise.

Yes, the choice is yours. After your TV fast has ended, you're free to watch as much or as little TV as you desire.

One thing is sure—such choices provide a window to our souls by revealing what we treasure in our hearts.

How's your celestial savings account?

BUT WAIT, THERE'S MORE!

1. If the woman in Arizona had purchased another television, how might such a purchase impact the communication between her and her husband? Would it strengthen it? Weaken it? Why?

2. Do you know somebody who, like this man, neglects his wife and/or family by spending too much time glued to the tube? If so, what might you say (perhaps from what you've learned during your TV-free month) to help this person get refocused on real-life priorities?

Spicy Speech

But now you must rid yourselves of all such things as these:
anger, rage, malice, slander, and filthy language from your lips.

COLOSSIANS 3:8

And now a word from our legal department . . .

If you visit New York, keep in mind it's against the law to shoot rabbits from a trolley car in motion. If Alaska is your destination, don't look at a moose from your airplane window. That, too, is against the law. And if you're planning on giving someone a box of chocolates in Idaho, keep it under fifty pounds. You guessed it. Anything heavier is illegal.

You might say Kentucky is the "cleaner" state since their law requires all residents to bathe at least once a year.[5]

And finally in Florida there's a community that made it a crime for adults to publicly swear in the hearing of a minor.

Umm, okay.

What about the other way around? Why isn't it also illegal for minors to assault the public with salty speech? You see, more often than not, it's been my experience that it's today's young people—not the adults—tossing around obscenities with the ease of a sailor.

Of course, many teens are exercising great verbal restraint and should be commended. But it seems that whether I'm standing in line at the grocery store, sitting in the stands at a ballgame, or walking through a mall, the perversity voiced by some young people would make Hugh Hefner blush. In fact, I've worked with students who are so "verbally challenged" that they appear incapable of completing a sentence without at least one #@!* expletive thrown in.

Actually, I'm not surprised by such verbal garbage flowing so freely.

Preteens and teens are exposed to a complete hard-core vocabulary through today's film diet. The elitist film industry insists on peppering the overwhelming majority of new movies with pungent speech.

A few years ago *Preview* (a bimonthly family film newsletter) included an analysis by editor Mark Perry of problematic language in popular films. Perry reported: "Out of the 209 movies *Preview* reviewed in 1996, 91 percent had crude language, 83 percent obscenities, and 73 percent regular profanity. Further, we were only able to find 14 (less than 7 percent) that didn't contain any crude words, obscenities, or regular profanities."

He adds, "Unfortunately, this problem shows every sign of becoming a trend. . . . We've reviewed 89 films [in 1997] and found *only four* without some form of foul language."

With that in mind, let's go back to the matter of our good-intentioned legislators in Florida. Will a law against public profanity get at the root cause? Frankly, I'm not convinced that's the answer. After all, doesn't public profanity have its roots in the home? Shouldn't Christian parents be raising a higher standard with their young people?

I'd like to know whatever happened to good, old-fashioned "fire-engine-red pepper"? My mother never hesitated to reach for that sharp spice when we DeMoss kids verbally strayed. She'd apply a healthy dose directly onto our tongues. I can assure you the taste of red pepper lingered well after I uttered the "s" word—you know: *Stupid!*

Okay, that was back when *stupid, idiot, jerk,* and *darn* were still on the offensive language list.

Thanks to Mom, as a preteen if my brain was slow to comprehend the importance of proper speech, my tongue would never forget the message. Mom's use of pepper or even soap sounds harsh, right?

Not really.

Look again at today's passage. The apostle Paul writes, "You must rid yourselves of all . . . filthy language from your lips." Do you see the use of that bothersome little four letter word *must*? Does that sound like Paul is making a *suggestion* regarding "filthy language"? Check out *must* in any dictionary. It's defined as "something indispensable, a requirement."

Mom was simply doing her best to follow Paul's orders.

Sad to say, thanks to the potty mouth of Bart Simpson, *South Park*, *Married with Children*, and a host of prime-time TV shows, society rarely frowns on profane banter. On the contrary, it *encourages* such expressions.

Of particular concern is the temptation for Christian parents to give up on this aspect of personal development with their children. One Christian associate, in an attempt to jokingly dismiss this as a discipleship issue, commented, "Bob, let's face it—God saves the tongue last!"

Does He?

Read what the apostle James said: "If anyone considers himself religious and yet does not keep a tight rein on his tongue, he deceives himself and his religion is worthless" (1:26).

BUT WAIT, THERE'S MORE!

1. If we're commanded to watch our tongues, why do we have such relaxed attitudes when profanity assaults us through television shows and the movies we rent?

2. How's your supply of red pepper? In this politically correct era, is it still a worthy idea to wash out the mouth of a family member who swears?

3. Did you know that for less than $150 several companies offer a "curse blocker" that bleeps out offensive words from your television and video rentals?

Busting Blockbuster

Are they ashamed of their loathsome conduct?
No, they have no shame at all;
they do not even know how to blush.

JEREMIAH 6:15A

When Friday night rolls around, what does your family usually do for fun? Watch TV? Rent a movie? Play a game? Work on a hobby?

When I was growing up, Friday night was officially designated as "Game Night" in the DeMoss household.

Bedtimes were extended.

Popcorn was popped.

Ice cream was dipped.

And our family would settle in for an evening of laughter, togetherness, light competition, and fun. Frankly, given the media-charged world in which we live, a family playing games together seems so, well, old-fashioned. (I hope you've been able to rediscover the joy of playing games during your TV fast.) Don't get me wrong. As I mentioned in chapter 3, from time to time our family enjoys having a "dinner theater" where we intentionally eat our meal while watching a movie.

Today, sad to say, home library shelves formerly lined with well-worn games have been replaced with rows of video tapes. Not wanting to miss a piece of the action, the nation's leading video rental store, Blockbuster Video, had an ad campaign that asked the question, "Why not make it a Blockbuster night?"

Seems the American masses have caught the vision.

Today renting a video is the entertainment of choice for millions.

But given the direction Blockbuster is headed with its selection, I'm beginning to wonder, "Why, indeed?"

In the past I've praised Blockbuster's family-friendly video renting procedures. For instance, they promise parents not to rent R-rated videos to minors. And they've refused to carry X-rated titles. These commendable policies are largely responsible for their incredible growth. System-wide revenues are in the multiple *billions*.

But with its extraordinary growth, I believe Blockbuster has lost sight of what made the company great—a wide selection of *family* fare. Here's what I noticed during a recent visit to my local Blockbuster, as well as while reviewing Blockbuster's web site.

Blockbuster has reversed itself on several controversial titles it previously refused to carry, including the despicable *The Last Temptation of Christ*. Many video covers, especially in the comedy section, featured women in various stages of undress. And without a blush Blockbuster boasts more than seventy *Playboy* or *Penthouse* titles and in excess of 740 graphically violent slasher films, including *Faces of Death*. Just walking through the aisles of their store made me feel the need for a bath.

Afterward I remember reading Jeremiah 6:15a. Here God's wrath was stirred against Israel because they had no shame and had lost the ability to blush. The thought struck me, *How about me? Am I honoring God with my viewing choices? Am I willing to turn off a video rental because "I didn't know it would be this bad"? Am I still capable of being embarrassed, or am I too jaded?*

As a black pastor friend says, "If ya can't say amen, then say ouch!"

By the way, while I was conducting my research at Blockbuster, a little girl—maybe six years of age—was with her mother in the next aisle. I overheard her asking her mom, "Why are those videos rated 17+?"

Good question.

In fact, until Blockbuster returns to their family-friendly roots, I, for one, won't be making it a Blockbuster night.

BUT WAIT, THERE'S MORE!

1. Why are videos with inappropriate language, sexual situations, and violence so popular—even among Christians? Have we lost the ability to blush?

2. The next time you consider selecting a video to rent, ask yourself: "Would I be embarrassed or ashamed if Jesus walked into my room as I watched this tape?"

Tempting Temptation

Be self-controlled and alert.
Your enemy the devil prowls around like a roaring lion
looking for someone to devour.

I   PETER   5 : 8

My wife and I own a small piece of secluded, undeveloped real estate. The first time we saw the tall, mature oak trees spreading their massive limbs skyward on the land, we knew this would be a great place to build our dream home.

We made an offer.

Signed the papers.

Shook hands.

And now we're waiting. We're in a holding pattern (to borrow a phrase from the airlines) until the city provides the sewer service.

Meanwhile, I built a cozy little workshop on the property. It's a modest space where I can get away and write. There's no bathroom. No refrigerator. No running water. But it's got a great view and enough electricity to power my laptop.

I'll never forget one evening when I was working well into the night on this book. As I pulled up the gravel road after a dinner break back at home, the sky appeared darker than usual. The moon remained hidden behind a cloud cover that resembled a shroud. Even the city lights, which normally keep me company, were barely visible.

I felt very alone—which, after all, I was.

That's when the shrieking started.

It began as a chorus of yelps. Within moments the yelps turned to blood-curdling howls. Instantly, the hair on the back of my neck stood up. I had never heard anything so inexplicably frightening.

What was it?

There was nothing I could do as this sound drew closer to my little shack. I felt like one of the Three Little Pigs. I held my breath as the Big Bad Wolf was about to blow down my house.

Just as quickly as the chaos had started, it stopped. Everything was perfectly silent—except my pounding heart.

Several friends live nearby. I grabbed the phone and called Jeff.

"Yeah, I heard 'em, too. Those were coyotes. They're kind of a wolf-dog mix with razor-sharp teeth. Be careful, Bob. They're very fast. Even killed a horse in the neighborhood. Oh, and they killed the neighbor's dog the other day."

Oh, great. We bought a piece of jungle property.

Several days later Jeff stopped by to let me know he was planning to try out a "wounded bunny" tape. A good way to kill coyotes, he explained, was to play a recording with the sounds of an injured rabbit. Coyotes prefer small game. The "promise" of an easy meal was virtually irresistible. When they approached the decoy, Jeff would shoot them from his back porch. Bingo. No more coyote problem.

You mean, you intentionally plan to beckon a pack of crazed coyotes to your house? I wondered. Seemed to me that he was exposing himself unnecessarily to something that might harm or even kill him. Yet Jeff, a seasoned hunter, knew precisely what he was doing. (I think he waited on the second-floor balcony.)

As I returned to my writing, I couldn't shake the feeling that there was a lesson for me in all of this. That's when today's Scripture passage came to mind. Here Peter describes the enemy of my soul as one who "prowls around like a roaring lion looking for someone to devour."

Much like those coyotes, Satan is poised to devour anyone he can sink his teeth into. He scopes out my weaknesses. He circles until he finds the pathway of least resistance. He's always roaming—looking for the right time to strike.

Knowing that you and I are the target of his threat, is it wise to let down our guard and allow Satan and his deeds of darkness into our home? He has more than one way of attacking, but inappropriate television-viewing is certainly near or at the top of the list.

"But, Bob, I know what I believe. I can handle his attacks! I'll never let a TV show become the passageway by which Satan gains access to my thought life."

Really?

This is where my analogy breaks down. Unlike Jeff the hunter who could bait coyotes, there's *never* a reason for us to tempt the tempter. In fact, as we learned previously, you and I are warned, "So, if you think you are standing firm, be careful that you don't fall!" (1 Cor. 10:12).

Personally, on the rare days when I watch television, my guard is up. I'm on the alert. I've learned from experience that I cannot trust most television programmers. And I'm prepared to change channels or turn the box off at the first sign of anything that might tempt me.

How about you?

BUT WAIT, THERE'S MORE!

1. In Luke 22:40b Jesus urged His disciples, "Pray that you will not fall into temptation." In light of this, how wise is it to pray for a pure heart, for example, and then view hours of TV programs that mock purity?

2. What's the best weapon you and I possess to defend against the devil's schemes?

3. If you were Satan, what would you do to mess someone up?

Genuine Imitation

Dear friend, do not imitate what is evil but what is good.

3 JOHN 11

Actor Peter Sellers is perhaps best known for his role as the dimwitted Inspector Clouseau in the Pink Panther film series. Bombs, bullets, and bimbo assassins always found their attacks backfiring. Clouseau was simply unstoppable. Sort of the Mr. Magoo of detectives.

A lesser-known Sellers classic was *Being There,* which, although I can't recommend the film due to one inappropriate scene, made a strong anti-television statement. In the film Sellers played the part of Chauncey Gardiner, an orphan who never left his home and who learned virtually everything he knew from TV. He parroted people from television.

So when I bought my first parrot, a beautiful blue and gold macaw, I just had to name him Chauncey. How perfect.

There are several things you must know about owning a large bird—especially a blue and gold macaw. First, they're very social. In fact, they "think" they're people. They love to have their head, belly, and under their wings scratched.

They love to shake hands, um, claws.

They give you kisses—sort of. (A bird has no lips.)

They enjoy taking a shower with you.

And rather than stick to a boring diet of seeds, they eat everything you and I eat—pizza, pasta, fruit, eggs, French fries—even chicken.

Unlike a dog, cat, or most other American pets, a healthy macaw can live upwards of sixty to eighty human years. You guessed it. You've got to include them in your will!

Most important, you and those who visit your home must watch what you say around a parrot. For example, we never said, "Shut up!" Imagine being on the phone talking to your boss, and in a quiet moment your bird shouts out, "Shut up!"

Not good.

Although most of their learning comes from the frequent repetition of words or sounds, a macaw can occasionally hear something just once, and the word becomes a part of its vocabulary. I remember being frustrated by Chauncey's squawking fit one Saturday afternoon while I was trying to take a nap. I raced to his cage and shouted, "Knock it off, you bad bird!"

I said the phrase just one time.

Guess who never forgot.

Owning a parrot is a good way to get an idea of the kinds of words spoken at home. They learn by listening to us. In addition to the basics ("Hello!" and "Pretty bird!") Chauncey's favorites were "I love you!" and "Give me kisses!"

There's one other tip to keep in mind if you're ever planning to get a macaw, African Gray, or Double Yellow Head Amazon (which are the best talkers). Unless you want your bird to swear like a sailor—which is *not* funny—keep it out of earshot of the television.

Why? You don't want the prime-time potty mouths putting words in the mouth of your $2,000 bird.

Which begs the question: "Why do we expose our dear children—and ourselves—to the same bad language we wouldn't subject a bird to? What might they be learning to parrot? Aren't our precious children worth much more than a bird?"

The apostle John challenges us to imitate "what is good." That verse suggests that we fill our minds with praiseworthy sights and sounds, which is why our family has the policy that our TV is not allowed to say or display things we should not say or display.

What's the policy in your home?

BUT WAIT, THERE'S MORE!

1. Prime-time sitcoms frequently show unmarried persons engaged in premarital sex. Studies prove that the consequences of such actions are rarely portrayed—such as contracting a sexually transmitted disease. Why do you think producers ignore consequences of such behavior?

2. The best way to imitate what is good is to embrace the challenge of 2 Corinthians 10:5: "Take captive every thought to make it obedient to Christ." Are the models your family views on TV or in a video worthy of imitation?

3. Children—even adults—look up to role models, both from real life and on TV. Is Jesus seen as our greatest role model?

It's the Real Thing

I have come that they may have life,

and have it to the full.

JOHN 10:10B

Atlanta is a "happening" town. Great restaurants. Underground jazz spots. Friendly people. Decent climate.

It's the home of the Braves.

And home, thanks to Dr. John Pemberton, to a little company called Coca-Cola.

Dr. Pemberton?

Yeah, he's the guy who invented Coca-Cola back in May of 1886. What's an invention without a catchy name? It was Pemberton's bookkeeper (a fellow named Frank Robinson) who came up with both the name and the now-famous Coca-Cola typeface that graces Coke products.

Sales bubbled with potential.

But having sold a mere nine drinks a day on average, Coke's first-year profits were flat. Through creative bottling and a series of imaginative advertising slogans, the Coca-Cola Company managed to put the fizz into their bottom line. Today more than one billion Coca-Cola products are consumed *each day*, making Coca-Cola the world's leading beverage company.

As you might guess, success breeds imitation.

Do you remember the "Cola Wars"?

During the early 1980s, second-place Pepsi staged a string of highly successful taste tests pitting Pepsi against Coke. Caps down, Pepsi won. While Coke foamed at the mouth, Pepsi gained market share by defining a new breed of thirsty souls—The Pepsi Generation.

In a move to fend off rival Pepsi's bid for the leading cola product, Coke countered by launching the catchy jingle, "It's the real thing."

Implication: Pepsi was an impostor.

For Coca-Cola it was a sweet move. If sales figures are any indication, Coke reigns supreme. Why? When it comes to refreshment, most folks want "the real thing."

Unfortunately, when it comes to living life, many of these same folks tend to reach for an imitation. For hours upon hours many prefer to embrace the synthetic world of TV than to engage in the real thing.

For the most part, we don't take extended walks in the park—or around the block. We don't get grass stains on our pants from rolling around in the backyard. We've forgotten the smell of burning leaves in the fall. We haven't climbed a tree or dreamed of building a tree fort . . . no way.

We like the imitation better. Right?

Not so fast. Not everyone has allowed the imitation to crowd out the real thing. Actually, there's a growing movement of radical types who dare to get a life—which now includes you.

Take Cindi. She lives with her husband and two boys in Franklin, Tennessee. She told me, "About sixteen years ago, I threw our television out the second-floor window to the concrete drive below when I came home to find a violent show on and my three-year-old in front of it. Yes, perhaps I snapped momentarily—but it certainly left an impression! For the remainder of our boys' lives, there was no TV. Instead, we had a life."

Just what did they do instead?

Cindi says, "We hiked, rode bikes, read books together, played games, talked, and fought(!)—but what we *didn't* do was subtly exchange *real lives* for virtual ones."

I love that: "Exchange real lives for virtual ones."

Excellent insight. I wish I had thought of it.

Cindi was quick to point out that "we are not a perfect family as a result. But we have *significant* relationships with one another. At the very least, sixteen years' worth of garbage wasn't deposited into our brains."

Don't get me wrong. My family still *owns* a television. But we're working to keep it from *owning* us.

BUT WAIT, THERE'S MORE!

1. Jesus said He came so that we might have life—and enjoy this new life to the fullest. How might accepting TV's imitation prevent us from savoring the beauty built into God's amazing creation?

2. The key word in our discussion of real versus imitation is *balance*. How do you know when you've watched too much?

3. Do you think watching the gardening channel is in any sense a satisfactory substitute for actually growing tomatoes or planting petunias in your yard?

How's the Water?

I have hidden your word in my heart
that I might not sin against you.

PSALM 119:11

Dad and Mom lived in the Philadelphia area for most of my life.

Same house.

Same phone number.

Same neighbors.

Same church. Nice.

But to live in the Philadelphia area required that they brave ice storms and massive snowdrifts in the winter, dodge man-eating potholes in the spring, and endure blazing heat and humidity in the summer.

Fall was nice—until the autumn leaves blanketed the lawn.

Who could blame them for moving to sunny Florida after thirty-plus years?

Once down there, Dad called to announce that he and Mom would be buying a house with—get this, a swimming pool. If you knew my dad, you'd understand why that announcement was such a shock to all of us. I remember how Dad would snicker at pool owners because of the endless work necessary to maintain a pool.

The annual spring cleaning, scrubbing away moss with acid.

A fresh coat of paint every three years.

Hassles with clogged filtering systems.

Skimming leaves and assorted bugs from the surface—daily.

Changing the burned-out underwater lamps.

Not to mention applying the proper number of chlorinating tablets, the water bill, and cost of supplies. Adding to the shock was that Dad's modest new pool was *heated* to a most comfortable 90 degrees. That way, he explained, if the outside temperatures dropped to 75 (which is Florida's version of freezing), they could still bask in the water.

This I had to experience. My family and I visited over Christmas in 1999. Upon arrival we kissed the folks, slipped into our suits, and made a splash. My daughter Carissa was the first one in.

"How's the water?" I asked.

"Very, very warm," came the reply.

I've learned I can't always trust Carissa's perspective. Why? She has fish blood. But in this case she was right.

More often than not, however, her idea of "warm" and mine were very, very different. You see, at one time we had lived next to a community pool. (Actually, during the summer Carissa lived *in* the pool and came home for meals.) Whenever I'd get an opportunity to swim, I'd head over to the pool to be the "monster" and chase Carissa underwater. But before I'd jump in, I'd ask my daughter, "How's the water?"

Inevitably she'd say, "It's great! Jump in!"

The first (and only) time I took her word for it, I jumped and nearly got frostbite. Within an instant of making contact with the water, my breath left my chest, and my skin turned blue.

You've probably had a similar experience. Someone who's been in the water for any length of time gets acclimated to the temperature. The body adjusts to the water temperature, and before long that person can't tell you if it's really cold, warm, or hot. You need a standard to know for sure—such as your big toe or, preferably, a thermometer.

In a way, this is analogous to what happens when we watch TV for any length of time. Our minds and our values get "used to" the material that, like a cold splash in the face, might have offended us at first but now seems commonplace.

That's why it's always risky to ask someone else for an opinion about a given show. The person may have been in the water too long and won't give you a realistic picture.

What's the best way to test the TV waters before jumping in? King David suggests that to avoid a moral belly flop, first dive deeply into the Scriptures. Fill your lungs with God's words and hold them inside ("I have hidden your word in my heart"). When you resume television viewing down the road, let God's commandments serve as your unswerving thermometer. Allow His Spirit to keep you from drifting into a sea of compromise so that, as David said, you might not sin against God.

(And, by the way, congratulations on completing three weeks!)

BUT WAIT, THERE'S MORE!

1. Have you ever rented a movie or selected a TV show based on a mild rating, only to be shocked at the actual contents? What does that reveal about the standards of those who formulated the ratings? Do they share your values?

2. According to Psalm 119:104-105, what are two added benefits to the study of Scripture?

3. Reflect for a moment: Have you or your family found yourselves more tolerant of some TV material that you once would have refused to view? If so, might this be an indication that you are getting used to the "water temperature"?

Use It or Lose It

I will repay you for the years the locusts have eaten.

JOEL 2:25

I love a good game of racquetball. It's a manly-man game. Unlike the more sedate sports (such as golf), racquetball pushes you to the very limit of physical exertion since the action is virtually nonstop for an entire hour.

About fifteen years ago I flew to Nashville on business from my home in Pittsburgh. On the last day of my trip a good buddy, Jim Thomas, heard I was in town and challenged me to play at the YMCA where he was a member.

Great! Let's do it. Six A.M.? No problem.

Typically racquetball is played on a "best-out-of-three" set. Jim won the first round. I took the second. We were well into the third game, and the competition was fierce. He's a very good player. But, as I recall, I was ahead in the final round. (Jim might have a different memory.)

Though tired and sore, I summoned the inner strength to pour it on. I served the ball. Jim returned it low and to my far right, requiring me to dive forward in order to make the shot. As I lunged toward the front wall, I felt this unbelievable sharp pain erupting on the back side of my left calf. For a moment—as I dropped to the floor—I thought Jim had hit my leg with his racquet to prevent my play.

Neither of us knew what had happened.

With a hobble, I managed to stagger off the court and onto a plane back to Pittsburgh. The next day the doctor explained that I had completely ruptured my Achilles tendon—big time. My condition was serious. We had to operate immediately. Can I assure you that a torn Achilles tendon is something I wouldn't wish on my worst enemy?

After the successful reconstruction, I was required to wear a cast up over my left knee for something like four months. In short, my life raced to a roaring stop. For starters I needed crutches and a wheelchair to move around.

Take a shower? Forget about it.

Doctor's orders—don't get the cast wet.

I had to stick my cast inside a plastic bag and hang it outside the tub while sitting on a chair for a time-consuming sponge bath.

After the cast was removed, six months of therapy and rehab began. During my first return visit to the doctor, he laid me out on a table, greased my left leg, and then applied a series of electrodes to various parts of my calf.

"Bob, we're gonna apply a little electricity to stimulate the muscles," he said with a calm, cool, detached voice.

Hold on . . . *Time out!* Electricity?

My mom always warned me not to put my finger in an outlet or a light bulb socket. Don't drop a radio in the bathtub water. You might get electrocuted!

"So, doc, what's this about intentionally throwing an electrical charge into my leg?"

He patiently explained that my leg muscles had atrophied from four months of disuse. Just like neglecting a foreign language you learned back in high school or failing to practice an instrument learned as a child, what we don't use, we lose. Inactive muscles break down. The increased levels of electricity would force my muscles to get the required exercise needed to regain their strength.

He was right. I'm happy to report that I've been able to return to the sport.

Funny how this difficult time in my life came to mind as I reviewed a common objection regarding the TV-turnoff experiment: "Bob, I just don't know what I'd do without the television."

Put it this way. People who have been spoon-fed TV's prepackaged entertainment over the years now suffer from "creative atrophy" of the mind. They've surrendered the task of personal imagination, thought, dreaming, and doing to a steady stream of phosphorous dots dancing in the TV monitor. The prospect of finally thinking for one-self becomes, well, *scary*.

I can appreciate that feeling. In my case, if I ever wanted to walk again, my system needed a healthy shock to jump-start it. Likewise, if you find yourself suffering from atrophy of the brain, don't despair. The condition can be corrected. Before long, and without the dis-traction from TV's trancelike grip, you'll find yourself emerging from this TV-induced zombie state.

You'll rediscover the joy of conversation.

Of actually *listening* to your spouse or children.

Of storytelling. Of play, laughter, and self-expression.

You see, the Lord promised the prophet Joel that He would restore what "the locusts have eaten" if the people of God repented. Back then, the locusts robbed God's people of His many blessings by destroying everything in their path.

Am I stretching matters to say television is a modern-day metaphor for locusts? I don't think so. It, too, robs us of the rich blessings God intends for us. TV sucks our imaginations dry, and it eats away our time.

Yet God's healing hand is extended to those who repent and desire His best.

BUT WAIT, THERE'S MORE!

1. Someone once said that we are most like our Creator when we create. When was the last time you tried your hand at painting with water colors, gardening, learning a musical instrument, or baking bread?

2. During your thirty-day TV-free experience, surround yourself with activities that stimulate the mind. Need help getting the cre-ative juices jump-started? Take your search to Amazon.com or BarnesandNoble.com. Both offer dozens of resources to choose from, such as the best-selling *365 TV-Free Activities You Can Do with Your Child* by Steven Bennett.

Greed Feeder

What causes fights and quarrels among you?
Don't they come from your desires that battle within you?

JAMES 4:1

The island of Madagascar lies just off the east coast of Africa. In this tropical paradise lives a rare creature, the ring-tailed monkey—or more precisely, a lemur. Never seen one? Just imagine a monkey whose face resembles a raccoon, whose body is the size of a large cat, and whose dainty hands are almost squirrel-like.

That's him. He'd make a wonderful Beanie Baby.

This cute little fellow has a tail that is typically longer than his body. He's on the endangered species list. And the zoologists who trap lemurs to place them in the safety of zoos say they're one of the most difficult animals to catch.

That's probably because these zoologists failed to ask the locals for help. For years the natives have had an effortless time catching these nimble creatures. What's their secret? Simple. They know two things about lemurs.

Melon seeds are their favorite food.

And these furry fellows are g-r-e-e-d-y.

Armed with this inside knowledge of monkey psychology, the natives set a creative trap. They take a melon and cut a hole barely large enough for the hungry critter's hand to reach in and grab the seeds. Being greedy, the monkey grabs as many yummy seeds as his little fist will hold before removing it. That's it.

But wait—how is that a trap?

Since the size of the hole barely permitted his paw entry, the monkey cannot take his hand out unless he first drops the seeds. This, of course, he refuses to do. His greed won't let him! Instead, the monkey fights with the melon—sometimes for hours—all the while screeching with displeasure over something he cannot obtain. He's a victim of his desire for gratification. While the lemur is distracted by this harmless ploy, the natives freely approach and nab him before he knows what happened.

I think it's fair to say television works in the same way—especially with younger children. How? Just as the monkey loves melon seeds, children love to watch TV—and lots of it. Just as the monkey is greedy for all of the seeds he sees, a child who watches too much television tends to become greedy for the endless "cool stuff" they see advertised on television.

So when Mom and Dad refuse to buy them the latest Grand Slam Johnny action figure or other must-have knickknack, they fuss and whine and throw a hissy fit. They, like the monkeys, refuse to let go of the desire for more things. Essentially, TV feeds people's greed.

Cheryl, a mother of four children in Kentucky, has witnessed this greed-trap dynamic in a unique firsthand way. She begins:

We turned our TV off two years ago (with the exception of a few videos and PBS). Since then we've experienced many benefits. In addition to the peace of mind at knowing that my children are protected from the negative impact of media, we talk more, play together, and read a lot.

I'm sure you have experienced similar benefits in your turnoff experience. But looking closer, Cheryl noticed a more subtle benefit of her family's TV-free policy. She continued:

Another mother asked me how I have trained my children to not want so many toys and beg for new things. Truthfully, I have not trained in this area! All I can guess is that since we have been TV-free for more than two years, the kids don't have the constant bombardment of commercials prompting them to want what they don't have.

As the saying goes, "Monkey see, monkey do."

While there *are* worthwhile television options, you and I need to be aware: The dangers of discontentment and desire are packed into every commercial break. The ads scream: "Buy me!" "Spend more!" "You just gotta get this!"

Greed—the desire to possess what we do not have—is a very real temptation for children and adults alike. In fact, the apostle James states that it's our "desires that battle within" us that lead to the "fights and quarrels" among us.

Do you want to reduce the family quarrels over acquiring more stuff? Don't let commercials on TV feed the greed.

How can you keep from falling into the greed trap?

Cutting back on television is a great place to start.

BUT WAIT, THERE'S MORE!

1. What's the best antidote for wrongful desires? King David says, "Delight yourself in the LORD and he will give you the desires of your heart" (Psalm 37:4). How do you "delight" in the Lord?

2. In most cases, our family hits the mute button whenever the commercials interrupt our program. Yet the program content itself might be a source of unhealthy desires, too. What's the best way to guard against that enticement?

Space Invader

The thief comes only to steal and kill and destroy.

JOHN 10:10A

During the summer of 1999, my family and I lived in a quaint country home. My best guess is that the house was originally built at least eighty years ago.

Translation: no insulation.

One small bathroom.

Uneven floors that creaked in protest every time you walked on them.

It had an unfinished dirt crawl space underneath that housed broken bottles, used tires, and even a used kitchen sink—perfect playground for the ever-present roaches and mice, I might add.

Oh, did I mention the chicken coop out back? About fifteen feet behind the house our landlord had an old barn—and I do mean *old*. The tin roof was sound, though heavily rusted. The walls suffered from a bad case of dry rot. And it had that slight "barn sag" prevalent in most older barns. A portion of this structure was rigged as a chicken coop for his chickens.

I was raised too much of a city slicker to have had much experience with chickens as a child. Somehow at the age of forty-one, I got the bug to buy a few of our own chickens—you know, as long as we were living next to a barn and coop.

I placed my order over the Internet. Several days later the chicks arrived—twenty-six to be exact. We read all about our baby Rhode Island Reds.

We fed them. We held them.

We chased them around. We had a blast!

Before long they were old enough to lay eggs.

Each morning my daughter Carissa or I would collect the fresh eggs and thank our chickens for their donations.

I remember one hot summer night, when my wife and I were sound asleep, the chickens launched into a blood-curdling squawking fit. Since our bedroom was within earshot of the coop, I bounded out of bed. Within seconds I slipped on my sandals, grabbed a flashlight, and headed out the back door.

Have you ever noticed how different things look in the dark?

Suddenly the ol' barn took on a sinister, foreboding air. I slowed my steps for a moment, contemplating the possible cause of this cry for help. A skunk? A snake? Or a dog? Maybe the chickens were just jostling for position on the roost.

As I stood outside the coop door in the dark, I confess my heart was racing. You've got to understand—inside, the coop was a dusty, spider-infested affair, draped with an endless array of antique cobwebs. Mice frequently scurried across the floor seeking a morsel of overlooked chicken feed. And one lone overhead forty-watt light bulb did what it could to cast a dim ray of light on the interior.

With my hand on the doorknob, my rationalizations began. Why bother to go in? Maybe it was nothing. The chickens would be fine. Whatever it was, surely it could wait until morning. Better to get some sleep.

Excuse, excuse, excuse. There's always a good excuse not to act.

Don't ask me why, but I pushed the door open and stepped in.

There in the center of the floor was a big, ugly possum munching on one of my chickens. He stopped his meal for a moment and stared at me. Frankly, I'm not sure who was more startled—me or the possum. Although I was too late for that poor chickie, I ran back to the house and grabbed my little target-practice pistol. No way would I stand by and let this invader harm my chickens. That was his last meal.

Farmer Bob to the rescue!

In a strange way I felt violated by the injustice of his invasion.

That possum had no business coming into our coop, spreading his fear and death. He was a thief. He didn't belong.

As I began work on this book, my mind drifted back to that experience and those feelings. Sometimes I get that same sense of violation from many of today's prime-time TV programs during the "family hour."

Think about it. You and I welcome TV into one of the most intimate places in our homes—our living rooms. There in the presence of our children this guest mocks our faith, uses profanity, and displays a complete disregard for the values we cherish.

Sure, there are exceptions. But for the most part, as someone once said: TV brings directly into our living rooms people and behaviors we'd never let past the front door.

Worse, while you and I might be quick to rescue a pet from an outside attacker—be it a chicken-eating possum or a neighborhood mutt making mincemeat of our cat—when it comes to TV, we make excuses for not taking action to guard our children and even ourselves against this socially acceptable thief. An invader, I might add, who frequently robs children of their innocence and drains the very lifeblood of creativity out of us.

You know, it felt good to defend my chickens.

How much more so when I defend my family.

It's certainly worth whatever it takes.

BUT WAIT, THERE'S MORE!

1. In my book *Learn to Discern* I identified ten defining characteristics of a critical thinker. One trait is: We recognize that those who create what we watch on TV—for the most part—don't share our values. Why do you think that is?

2. I knew what to do in order to prevent that possum from harming the rest of my chickens. Aside from shooting your TV, what might be a way to prevent it from causing harm in your home?

3. Boycotting the advertisers of problematic shows has been one effective strategy to reduce offensive programming. Can you think of other ways to influence what TV producers do?

The Silver-Screen Shuffle

Let not my heart be drawn to what is evil,
to take part in wicked deeds with men who are evildoers;
let me not eat of their delicacies.

PSALM 141:4

The other night my wife and I were slated to go out on "date night." That is no small accomplishment. With a family, you see, everything must be officially "scheduled," or it won't happen.

School plays.

Church activities.

Dental visits.

And date night. All family functions must find their place on the Master Calendar. Having crossed that ever-important first hurdle, our next task was to decide what to do.

Dinner and a bookstore visit? Could be relaxing.

Stroll the mall? A snoozer in my book.

See a movie? Is there anything really worth seven dollars a ticket?

How about a concert? After all, here in the Nashville area we have a number of live music options. In addition to big arena-style concerts, we have a host of small, intimate cafe settings where local aspiring artists perform.

We checked the local listings, but nothing grabbed us.

That's when I got the phone call. "Bob, there's this really awesome film you've got to see!"

"Funny, my wife and I were just wondering what to do."

"Yeah, and Joe Movie Critic says it's got his thumbs up. . . ."

Against my better judgment we headed out the door for dinner and this "must-see" movie. Dinner was delightful. My wife and I desperately needed the time to talk. Face to face. As husband and wife. With no kids and no interruptions.

One of us noticed the time. Oops. Almost 7:15 P.M.

If we were going to make the movie, we'd have to cut short the conversation and *run!* We paid the server, darted out the door, zoomed across town, found a place to park, rushed to the box office, plunked down $14.50 for two tickets, and then sprinted to our seats.

Whew! We made it. Barely. What an effort.

We've since called this race the "Silver-Screen Shuffle."

As the opening credits danced across the screen, my wife and I caught our breath. But what really took our breath away was the profanity that assaulted us within moments of the movie's opening. I'm no prude, but to wade through a dozen or so obscenities in the first ten minutes seemed pointless.

Did you know that at most theaters you can request a refund or movie credit for your ticket if you are dissatisfied? I'm not sure that's an option if you stay for the *entire* film. However, many managers want your business and will provide some form of reimbursement if you voice your concern early on.

That's exactly what we did. The theater issued two credits, and we headed home—disappointed once again with Hollywood. On hindsight both of us wished we had lingered over dinner. That, as it turned out, was the main attraction.

The next day I called that Christian buddy who told me it was a "must-see" flick and explained what had happened.

"Oh, yeah. Sure, there's a little profanity, but, hey, other than that, it was great! Beautiful scenery. A good plot—"

I had to interrupt him.

Let's pretend I've recommended a wonderful little restaurant to you. It's got comfortable chairs and a great view. The servers are attentive. The food is cooked to perfection. But I fail to tell you that they've got this nasty habit of spitting in your water, soda, or coffee before bringing it to your table. Wouldn't you wonder about my judgment? Wouldn't you want to know why I make excuses for such unacceptable behavior? And wouldn't you scratch your head about my continued patronage of such a place?

Yet this bizarre situation is a precise picture of how we relate to our film diet. A movie producer in effect spits on our moral position through unnecessary crassness or pointless profanity, and we don't do anything about it. On the contrary, some folks recommend such fare to unsuspecting patrons.

Why? Because far too many believers today fail to do as King David did. David longed for discernment. He craved righteousness. At one point in his life he begged God, "Let not my heart be drawn to what is evil."

No matter how appealing.

No matter how nice the package.

No matter how popular.

Furthermore he prayed, "Let me not eat of their delicacies."

In effect, David prayed, "Lord, help me to love what You love and hate what You hate."

As God grants us this request, our jaded hearts begin to soften. The blinders on our eyes fall away. Our feet gain new freedom to resist going to a bad film, play, or concert, or they walk out the door once we're there.

This has been *our* prayer.

Will you make it *yours*?

BUT WAIT, THERE'S MORE!

1. The theater provided us two passes for a future film. But it's been three months, and we still haven't found one worthy of our time. Why? Instead of relying on word-of-mouth, we now consult with several respectable Christian film-review services. I highly recommend *Plugged In* from Focus on the Family (1-800-AFAMILY) or *Preview* (1-800-807-8071) as a place to start.

2. Have you ever walked out of a movie due to objectionable content? If so, why? If not, why not?

Spare the Rod

Do not withhold discipline from a child;
if you punish him with the rod, he will not die.

PROVERBS 23:13

When you think of the word *discipline,* what comes to mind? I guess the answer depends on whether you're the provider or receiver of the discipline. If you had asked me that question when I was a child, I would have responded, "Tears—and a sore bottom."

Comedian Bill Cosby has one of the funniest sketches on discipline I've ever heard. He calls it "The Same Thing Happens Every Night." Cosby, in his side-splitting style, paints a picture of life with young kids after dinner. Everyone knows they're to take a shower. They know they're supposed to take turns and "use soap."

While he and his wife sit at the empty dinner table drinking coffee together, they listen to the muffled sounds of struggle as their children fight their way through the evening routine upstairs.

After a few moments one of his little cherubs will come downstairs to file a complaint. Soap in the eyes. A towel used to whip another's behind. Within seconds, all of the kids come down to voice their particular grievances.

It's the same thing every night, which prompts his wife to have a "conniption" at their misbehavior. She grabs a yardstick and announces, "Let the beatings begin!" Cosby explains his role: As the kids run for cover, he is the goalie—to "push the kids back into play."

After my wife and I had our first two kids, I understood why Cosby's story had such a ring of truth. We experienced the same thing—every night—which was no real surprise. Most of the books we read on Christian parenting underlined the place of, and need for, discipline.

We were told it was our duty. It was a package deal. Have kids— have discipline. Spare the rod—spoil the child.

Actually, discipline comes naturally for most of us guys. We men like structure. Order. Everything in its place. With military precision, we bark out the orders and expect compliance. Bed unmade? Missed a curfew? Sassy remark?

Bam!

The disciplinarian in us takes over, and we dish out the consequences.

But the longer I live and the older I become, the more I'm tempted to just "let it slide." Cut 'em slack. R-e-l-a-x. Chill out. Yes, the easiest thing for me to do would be to look the other way when my children disobey. Why?

For starters, I see so little discipline around me. A kid threatens to blow up his elementary school, and he gets two days off to "think about" his actions.

A child attacks another student on the school bus; he's slapped with a detention.

And, as any couch potato could tell you, few parents in TV land are pictured disciplining their young. If they do, rarely is it done in a healthy, measured manner. Let me take it a step further. Seldom are we viewers presented with a praiseworthy view of parenting in prime time, especially when the topic is discipline. If anything, it's the extremes that capture the air time—either a parent is abusive, or he's hands off.

I believe that the more we parents watch TV, the more likely we're tempted, perhaps at some subconscious level, to spare God's mandated rod on the "seat of understanding." It's such an out-dated practice.

So, as it were, un-hip.

Narrow-minded.

What's more, television teaches me that it's a "kids world" where youth are the smart ones, and we "old folks" (anyone older than twenty-something) are bumbling simpletons.

Take, for instance, Homer Simpson of *The Simpsons*. When Homer finally decides it's time to put his foot down on son Bart's delinquent behavior, Homer's either apologetic for imposing a penalty, or he explodes and overreacts. He's wishy-washy. It's safe to say that Homer is portrayed as a complete nincompoop.

A ninny.

Certainly a numskull.

But even worse than the absence of discipline on TV is the general lack of respect for authority figures in most sitcoms. Rudeness reigns. When our children take their cues on parental interaction from today's one-dimensional TV parents, they learn to mouth-off rather than respect and honor Mom and Dad.

Is it any wonder we parents want to take the pathway of least resistance?

But God didn't give us that option. Examine those words again: "Do not withhold discipline from a child."

To be sure, biblical discipline isn't just reading the riot act to unruly kids. It's really a lot closer to the concept of mentoring.

Isn't that, after all, how God disciplines us? He shepherds us as He conforms us into "the likeness of his Son" (Romans 8:29). He does not correct us with the anger of an uptight celestial drill sergeant. Rather, God is more like a personal trainer. He pushes us to do another lap in order to bring out the *best* in us.

It's been said that mentoring has three components—a shoulder to cry on, a listening ear, and a swat to the pants when needed. I may not see this biblical ideal reinforced in society or in the world of TV. Yet because of my love for God, I know there will be times when I must mentor my children—occasionally with that swift but loving swat to the behind.

Don't get me wrong. Discipline is never pleasant.

But listen to the payoff: "No discipline seems pleasant at the time, but painful. Later on, however, it produces a harvest of righteousness and peace for those who have been trained by it" (Hebrews 12:11).

BUT WAIT, THERE'S MORE!

1. Aside from the Waltons, can you name several adult TV characters who model a healthy view of discipline in the home?

2. Pretend you are a producer for a new family sitcom. How might your script demonstrate that choices have consequences?

3. When parents neglect to teach their children right from wrong, how does this failure impact society?

Let's Make a Deal

My brother Tim is what you'd call a serious trader.

Let me clarify.

He's a serious trader of *baseball cards*.

At last count Tim's personal collection hovered around 500,000 cards. No joke. His command of the various players, their personal statistics, and their relative card value is nothing short of astounding. Tim knows his stuff. He knows what to buy, when to buy it, and, most important, when to sell. One of his prized cards is a mint condition 1954 Ted Williams. Any good collector would place its worth in the ballpark of $1,000.

That's $1,000 for *one* baseball card.

I've done a little card collecting in my time—nothing on the scale of Tim. In the late eighties, inspired by my brother's success with collectibles, I proudly purchased several cases of Topps baseball cards. (A case is made up of twenty boxes. Each box contains thirty-six packs of cards. A pack holds fifteen individual cards.) In short, a case contains 10,800 cards.

I was now on my way to becoming a big-time dealer, or so I thought. It was with great anticipation that I called Tim ten years later to see how much the value of these cases had appreciated. After some hesitation he said, "Actually, Bob, they're worth *less* than you paid for them."

Huh? How could I be left holding the bag?

He explained that I had struck out on an industry curveball. The three major baseball card companies—Topps, Fleer, and Don Russ—had overproduced the number of cards, effectively flooding the market during the time I purchased my cases. Not to rub it in, he informed me that his one Ted Williams card was worth at least four such cases.

That's 43,200 of my cards for his one Ted Williams. Talk about a raw deal.

It pains me to remember that I exchanged something of real value (my cash) for what appeared to be of value (the cards). What am I going to do with thousands of cards nobody wants?

I share this experience with you because it illustrates why I became so motivated to get unhooked from my television set. Essentially, I came to the realization that my time spent watching TV, like those cases of cards, was a bad deal. No matter how I cut it, when it came to trading something of real value (my time) for what *appeared* to be of value (endless TV shows), I always got the short end of the stick.

Let's review the terms of this arrangement. For my part, when I trade my time for TV, I must suspend most of my body functions; I sit in a catatonic state; I don't speak to my wife or children—unless it's a commercial I don't care to see; I put my talents on hold; I will get no exercise that would otherwise enhance a healthy life; I won't accomplish any tasks around the house; I tend to munch on excess food. On top of all that, I must suppress my better moral judgment while the TV mocks my personal convictions and belief system.

What does TV give me in exchange?

A diversion? Some laughter?

A little relaxation?

That's it?

Is that the best trade I can get for my investment of time? Time, after all, is the most precious commodity of all. Everyone receives the same amount of "time" each day. You can't buy more time no matter how rich you are. And once you spend it, there's no way to repurchase it.

From now on when I trade my time, I plan to get my money's worth. Whether it's TV viewing or some real-life activity, I intend to maximize the experience. How about you?

BUT WAIT, THERE'S MORE!

1. Take a moment now to reflect on all that you give up for TV viewing. Then contrast that to the "benefits" you have received from TV. Has this been a good deal? Or has it been more like my baseball card purchase?

2. Let me suggest that you read again the familiar parable of the talents in Matthew 25:14-30. What is Jesus saying to you and me about maximizing the use of our God-given talents?

Be Your Own V-Chip

And this is my prayer: that your love may abound
more and more in knowledge and depth of insight,
so that you may be able to discern what is best
and may be pure and blameless until the day of Christ.

PHILIPPIANS 1:9-10

Have you ever heard a friend claim that something was true because "I just saw it on TV"? Many view TV as a reliable source of truth, of what is real, of what we can trust.

After all, you and I live in what many have called the "media age." As a product of this era, do you think you have the ability to discern the difference between fantasy and reality? Whenever I pose that question to a group of teens or adults, virtually all claim that they have no problem separating fact from fiction.

How about you? Let's see how you'd score on this two-question quiz.

Question number one: What is the first thing a police officer is supposed to do when making an arrest? If you answered, "Read them their rights," you'd be *wrong*. Why do we universally think that providing the Miranda rights during an arrest is the first responsibility of law enforcement agents? Probably because that's the way it's done on television and in the movies.

Evidently if we see something frequently enough—even if it's a falsehood—we accept it as fact. But, alas, Hollywood's embellishment of reality doesn't change reality. As a matter of fact, a policeman friend in California (who pointed out this fallacy to me) claims he is *never* required to read an arrestee his rights unless the officer plans to interrogate the suspect.

Okay, here's question two: Al Gore commented in 1999, when he was vice president, that Americans needed detailed content codes (such as "V"—violence, "S"—sexual situations, "L"—coarse language) along with the television ratings. Is he right or wrong?

If you answered, "Yes, we the public need specific content codes for television shows," I can understand why you might think so. After all, the U.S. Congress, the Federal Communications Commission, child advocacy groups, and even the President have told us we *need* them. Further, various senators have virtually demanded that broadcasters get their signals fine-tuned with clearer content codes.

Naturally, we the consuming public corporately nod in agreement that such a guideline would be helpful. But that's a mistake. I don't believe specific content codes are necessary. In fact, embracing the often-repeated fantasy that we need something because important public figures (including the President) say it's in our best interest, we can miss the reality of a much deeper issue.

For instance, why do so many programs today need to be rated in the first place? Did Americans phone Hollywood to request more violence, steamier sex scenes, and a greater peppering of profanity in prime time? How, then, did it get so bad right in front of our recliners?

The fact that we still bother to tune in at all begs yet another question: What does this tell us about our national appetite for sleaze, mayhem, and banal bantering? If we need anything, it is answers to those concerns. Instead, we've adopted the notion that we need these new TV-content codes.

So what's the answer? A V-chip—that little programmable electronic blocking device that restricts certain shows?

A Senate mandate?

Another unreliable and vague series of letters flashed briefly at the beginning of a show requiring a decoder ring to decipher?

I'd propose instead three simple steps:

1) Get to know a show. It takes only a little effort to identify the

"spirit" of a program's direction. For example, on the whole I've found that *Wishbone* is consistently entertaining, instructive, and positive viewing for children; *America's Funniest Home Videos* is known for innocent laughs, *Touched by an Angel* for its spiritual dimension; *Melrose Place* wallows in sexual carousing, and HBO's comedy spot is dominated by "comedians" who rely upon rapid-fire obscenities. A content code flow chart isn't needed.

2) Limit your choices. Make your task easier. When it comes to the world of TV, having more channels to choose from is not necessarily better—in fact, it's worse. The massive volume of choices causes us to become lazy in our attempts to identify where a show's producers are coming from. It's much easier to "monitor" four or five options than four or five hundred.

3) Learn to live without it. Just as you stop shopping at a store that routinely provides unsatisfactory service, why not look to alternative forms of entertainment if your television experience is so problematic? Why not play a game, listen to music, read a book, or engage in some meaningful conversation with family and friends?

By the way, since society seems bent on content codes, I've developed a few of my own: "DP"—disrespectful to parents, "SM"—smart mouth, "WG"—worthless gossip, and "NWMT"—not worth my time.

BUT WAIT, THERE'S MORE!

1. Can you trust the networks to know and label what your family finds offensive? Do you think that a member of the media elite assigned to rate a TV show—someone who most likely doesn't share your value system—will consistently provide reliable guidance?

2. When your family returns to whatever level of TV-viewing you decide is appropriate, consider limiting the spectrum of choices by canceling your cable and/or satellite service. This will make the job of decision-making much simpler. Fewer choices, fewer problems.

There Is a Season

There is a time for everything,
and a season for every activity under heaven.

ECCLESIASTES 3:1

In his delightful cartoon strip "Calvin and Hobbes," Bill Watterson captures the intimate conversations between six-year-old Calvin and his stuffed tiger Hobbes. As any child that age might do, Calvin views Hobbes as much more than a toy. He's Calvin's best friend and confidant. It's Calvin's imagination that brings Hobbes to "life."

If you haven't followed the series, Calvin is a typical child who loves to watch television and who frequently describes TV's appeal. By contrast, Hobbes is the skeptical voice of restraint, reason, and balance.

In one sketch Calvin and Hobbes are standing outside under a tall tree. Calvin, pointing to the big outdoors surrounding them, exclaims, "Look, Hobbes. This world is kind of like TV. A casual observer might even confuse the two. But if you notice, here the colors are less intense, and the people are uglier."

Hobbes listens patently.

Calvin checks his watch before continuing his analysis. "Also, I see that several minutes can go by without a single car chase, explosion, murder, or pat personal exchange."

Evidently real life is too boring for Calvin. In the final frame they're back indoors. Calvin is pictured slouching in his favorite stuffed chair in front of the television as Hobbes looks on with indifference.

Hobbes quips, "Why settle for less, hmm?"

"Shh. This is my favorite deodorant commercial," Calvin says, pointing to the tube.

I love the way Watterson makes his point. On the surface, when compared to television, real life appears to be, well, dull—especially for the video veggie who views deodorant commercials as something of value!

By now I trust that your TV-free trial has expanded your view of reality. You've probably come to see that there's much more to life than spending nights watching car chases, explosions, and "pat personal exchanges." That's the overwhelming verdict I've heard from those who, like you, have radically reduced their dependence on television in the home.

For example, Mary Ann from Newfield, New Jersey, observed in her family's journal, "It's been a great experience for our family. It opened my eyes and showed me how easy it is to adjust to no television." Among the numerous highlights from their experience (including an increased level of book-reading) she noted, "Amazing! I went downstairs to exercise, and Chris (the eleven-year-old) followed me down and exercised with me. He would have otherwise been playing with the Nintendo." She adds, "And the most amazing thing, Dennis (twenty years old) sat down at the piano and started playing—something he hasn't done in about a year!"

At the same time, TV has its place.

As King Solomon wisely observed, there is a season for all activities. The key concept Solomon has implied is "balance." Everything has its proper place. That's why, as you approach the end of your TV-free month, it's important to consider how you plan to schedule real-life activities with any future TV viewing.

On that issue Mary Ann from Newfield, New Jersey, admitted there were several occasions toward the end of their TV-free experiment when her kids counted down the days (3, 2, 1 . . .) until "we can watch TV again."

With just a few days remaining in your TV fast, your family might be in that countdown mode at this very moment. If so, now—while your perspective is still fresh—is the best time to evaluate and plan a workable viewing schedule, assuming you plan to return to some level of television usage.

Mary Ann and her husband, Ron, wisely crafted such a plan. She writes, "We made it! It went quite smoothly. I'm not ready to throw the TV away. But there *is* a new TV schedule posted at the TV set." Here's what they plan to follow:

Sunday	—	No TV
Monday	—	No TV
Tuesday	—	No TV
Wednesday	—	TV okay from after school until dinner
Thursday	—	No TV
Friday	—	TV after dinner
Saturday	—	TV until 11 A.M. and in the evening

Mary Ann adds, "Some exceptions will be made for family movies and the like. By the way, the boys came home from school somewhat excited to watch again. They turned on the TV for about an hour—and then turned it off!"

I guess those deodorant commercials weren't so fantastic after all.

BUT WAIT, THERE'S MORE!

1. Take a few minutes today to draft a family viewing schedule. You might want to start with what Ron and Mary Ann's family has proposed. Modify it according to your projected needs and interests.

2. Another important feature might be to devise a plan to get back on track should the family get out of balance with their viewing habits in the days ahead.

Watch What You Watch

A simple man believes anything,

but a prudent man gives thought to his steps.

PROVERBS 14:15

Can you believe that tomorrow is your final day of the TV turnoff? Tonight as I sat down to write, it dawned on me that these daily visits are almost over. With that in mind, there's one final perspective on TV and film viewing I must squeeze in.

And it's a bit tricky.

It has to do with what we *don't* see when we watch TV.

You see, when watching the tube, we voluntarily give over the control of our eyes and our mind to the producer of what we're watching. In other words, we will only see on TV what he or she wants us to see. It's the producer's values, priorities, and point of view that take center stage. In my book *Learn to Discern* I describe this phenomenon as "the directed eye."

And here's the rub: What we *don't* see can be as important as what we *do* see—or *more* important. Classic case in point: When the used car salesman tells you how great a particular car is, it's wise to consider, "What's he *not* telling me?" and "Why isn't he telling me the full story?" The same principle applies to TV.

For instance, I recall a report on the absence of religion in television land. Professors from three universities tracked some 100 shows featured on CBS, NBC, ABC, and FOX. Bottom line? They found that religious beliefs and practices rarely appeared. And, worse, when they did, most of the time such belief was portrayed in a negative light, especially during the evening news.

That means the couch potato who sits glued to the television and who believes "TV tells it like it really is" would rarely see people of faith pictured positively. Yet in reality the majority of Americans attend religious services at least once a week. So viewers have a skewed picture of faith in America.

Here's another example that may be more stunning. For years the Disney name has been synonymous with wholesome, family-oriented films. But a closer look at Disney's roster of animated motion pictures actually leaves me wondering if the company has something against motherhood. Moms are simply nonexistent in Disney films.

Let's look at Disney's routine exclusion of mothers from its cartoon classics. Think back to Aladdin. He didn't have a mother. Jasmine doesn't have a mother either. Nor does Ariel, Belle, or Pinocchio. In the case of Snow White and Cinderella, the closest they come is "wicked" stepmothers. Worse, Peter Pan doesn't have the foggiest notion of what a mother is! In the case of the *Hunchback of Notre Dame*, the bio-mom gets pushed out of the picture from the start.

Come to think of it, Sleeping Beauty's mother is only briefly referred to as "King Stefan and his queen." Don't forget *The Jungle Book*, in which Mowgli was an orphan. Poor Pocahontas was raised without a mother, too. And in the case of Bambi, he had a mother—but his mom got shot!

Not one of these pictures portrays two happily married, well-adjusted parents involved in their children's lives. Disney's situation is sort of like Murphy Brown's—but in reverse. In these pictures it's Dad holding down the home. Granted, in both *The Lion King* and *101 Dalmatians* we see two lions and two dogs who serve as parents. But these differ from the aforementioned animated features because the lead characters are *animals* rather than *people*.

So what's the big deal?

With Mom out of the picture, marriage takes another whack.

I don't want to sound overly picky by addressing this matter. I doubt it's some calculated conspiracy by the board at Disney Studios. It's just that this pattern of omission is conspicuous and difficult to explain—especially in light of the family-friendly image Disney commands.

There's an important reason to consider the implications of motherless Disney characters. Helping our family see that movies frequently fail to portray a healthy picture of reality is a small but vital step in their journey toward becoming critical thinkers. Given Disney's dwarfed track record of affirming motherhood, you have a host of examples with which to begin this learning process.

BUT WAIT, THERE'S MORE!

1. The next time you watch a movie or TV show together, discuss how the producers portray the family. Are there two happily married parents? Or are they divorced? Are the parents presented as wise and loving individuals? Or are they depicted as nincompoops?

2. Here's a question to ask of today's films: Does the picture of reality the producer presents represent what I know to be true from real life, or is it a distortion? If it's a distortion, why is the producer trying to manipulate reality?

AFTERWORD

Life Can Be Rosy Without Rosie

Let us throw off everything that hinders
and the sin that so easily entangles, and let us run
with perseverance the race marked out for us.
Let us fix our eyes on Jesus.

HEBREWS 12:1B-2A

Have you ever gone diamond-hunting?

I don't mean going to the mall in search of a deal on a diamond ring. I'm talking about grabbing a shovel, getting down in the dirt, and digging for a diamond in the rough.

I have.

Just call me Prospector Bob.

It was the summer of 1999, and my family was hungry for a really different vacation experience. Always one to try new things, I thought about taking a trip to the Crater of Diamonds State Park in Murfreesboro, Arkansas. I can't recall where I first learned about this extraordinary opportunity, but I jumped at the thought of finding gemstones in this open-to-the-public diamond park.

My next task was to convince my wife this would be "fun."

"Honey, did you know this is the only place in the world where you can hunt and keep all the gemstones and diamonds you find?" No response.

I tried another approach. "They say the first diamond was discovered in this thirty-five-acre site back in 1906. In fact, more than

70,000 diamonds of various sizes have been unearthed since that time. Imagine that!" She yawned.

"Babe, ever heard of the 'Uncle Sam' Diamond? It weighed 40.23 carats, and it was found in *this* park."

That got her attention.

"Yeah, plus the 16.37 carat 'Amarillo Starlight,' not to mention the 'Star of Arkansas,' which was a 15.33 carat rock! Plus, it says here that garnet, jasper, amethyst, opal, agate, and quartz stones have also been found."

That did it. We loaded up the Pathfinder and headed west.

Six hours later we arrived, watched the instructional video, rented the shovels, pans, and screens, and headed out into the massive open field of . . . dirt. My wife, our then twelve-year-old daughter Carissa, and I found a spot and dug in with a passion. Our plan was to spend three or four days foraging for the ultimate treasure.

A watchful sun began to beat unmercifully upon us.

Our sweat mixed with the dust.

Fingernails became caked with soil.

Blisters began to form on our hands.

Within twenty minutes it was time for a break.

While sipping sodas, we noticed one guy who took the task of prospecting *seriously*. He must have dug down at least six feet. Unlike our puny rented sand pails, this fellow had five-gallon buckets that he used to carry the earth to the cleaning station. That's where you screen and wash off the dirt in hopes of revealing a rare gemstone. I later learned that he came hunting for diamonds almost every day.

Talk about commitment.

Determination.

Willpower.

By contrast, I think we lasted a measly half-day before packing it in. We headed to the hotel with nothing more than sore backs and mud-caked shoes to show for our efforts.

Fair-weather prospectors. We canceled the rest of the dig and returned home.

Guess what? If you so choose, today marks the end of a TV-free life, and *you made it!* Unlike my family on that vacation, you toughed it out. I'm proud of you. In fact, let me be the first to applaud your commitment to go the distance. Against the odds and against circumstances that may have tempted you to give up, you've experienced something few people will ever try to discover.

It's something very special.

Something life-changing.

Something your family will never forget.

In the words of today's Scripture, you've run the race, a race to go deeper in your faith, and have persevered. Congratulations! Perhaps you feel like Leah from Wyoming, Michigan. After Leah took the TV-free challenge, she shared these thoughts with me:

I am a single person living on my own. Several months ago I completed the TV turnoff. Let me just say the turnoff had a profound impact on my life! It enabled me to recognize just how little I was living my life in accordance with what I wanted for myself in my walk with the Lord.

It also contributed to a job change. You see, when I finally got past the noisy, often mindless entertainment of television, I came to a realization of what I truly value and how I should be prioritizing my life. As a result of the TV turnoff, I am making much wiser decisions, which I am confident will revolutionize the way I would raise a family, should God bless me with one.

Leah mentioned that her TV-free month had had a "profound impact" on her. That's exactly what James and Debbie from Austin, Texas, and their three children experienced. At the conclusion of their journal, Debbie offered this insight:

The greatest gift to me of having the TV off has been the gift of time. Time for the kids to have a leisurely snack after school and then do homework instead of working to cram it in before or after favorite TV programs. Time created by sleeping more and therefore making my waking hours more productive. Time to savor and make the most of the final weeks of summer. Time for our kids to play with each other. Time for their imaginations to take hold and creatively express themselves.

I loved the way they ran laughing through the house and how all three spent countless hours sitting together playing cards, school, putting on puppet shows, and listening to audio tapes together. Today I told our older two (David and

Emily) how great it was that they had spent so much of their time working on things of value—their relationships with each other, instead of sitting in front of the TV squandering their time.

In the case of Richard and Julie from Bloomsburg, Pennsylvania, a full week after their family of five finished the fast, Julie reported:

Well, Bob, there are a few pleasant surprises. After the initial joy at being able to watch TV, I've noticed we don't turn the TV on automatically anymore. In fact, it's much more of an annoyance during the course of a day than anything else. Usually the TV doesn't come on until after supper, homework, baths, etc. And that's NOT because of a new rule or anything like that! It's simply because a pattern has been broken. Now that we don't "need" TV, we are much more particular about what and when we watch.

You're at a crossroads. Before slipping back into the old habit of a TV-dominated schedule, savor what you've learned. Just as these families paused to reflect upon the benefits of their TV-free month, why not do the same? Did your family find the time away from television worthwhile? While you're at it, consider what, if any, were the losses. Are you glad you took the challenge? Would you recommend it to others? As a matter of fact, drop me a note. I'd love to hear how things went for your family (my address is at the end of the book).

ONE YEAR AND STILL COUNTING

As you ponder the future role of TV in your home, I thought you might enjoy hearing from some who weighed the "pros" and "cons" of television usage and chose to remain TV-free for several additional months—in some cases, for many years.

Although my family and I have elected to use the TV on a selective and strictly limited basis in the DeMoss household, I personally admire those "TV-free veterans" who have made that choice. They have discovered life can be rosy without Rosie:

Melinda, Ash Grove, Missouri: *Our family has been TV-free for a year and a half, and we think it's wonderful! The first month was actually a bit difficult because it was like getting over an addiction. We didn't know what to*

do or how to entertain ourselves apart from television. I'll admit we had become
dependent on the "mindless entertainment" provided by our TV.

Now, eighteen months later with a TV-free home, we have no desire to
invite the TV back into our lives. Our family is closer, and the house is just more
peaceful without "that negative force" invading our space.

Joseph and April, Atlanta, Georgia: *It was back in 1987 that our TV*
went out the door. Our son had just turned five. We thought we could control what
he watched, but we quickly learned that was impossible. He'd turn the dial the
moment we left the room. Even when we sat with him to watch together, we
couldn't control what they'd flash on the TV screen, so out it went. By twelve years
later we've met hundreds of families who, like us, don't own a TV. My son, by
the way, is an avid book-reader. (We've been to the library so often that the librar-
ian knows us by name!) He's even taught himself how to play the piano.

We realize television has some good programming in between the bad stuff.
But that's like making your favorite sandwich, placing it in a baggie, and then
throwing it into the garbage can. Would you go in and dig through the garbage
to get it out, or would you go and eat somewhere else? That's the way we feel
about TV. There's just too much garbage to dig through for the little good. We
don't even miss it.

Tim and Jennifer, Philadelphia, Pennsylvania: *We totally gave up the*
use of television in our home three years ago, and we did it cold turkey. In fact,
we sold our television and donated our VCR to our church. We tried not to make
a big issue of telling anyone (and still don't) because we don't want to come
across as somehow more spiritual for our decision.

When our choice does come up in conversation, we get mixed responses.
Some responses are what we feared: "Oh, aren't you super-spiritual" and the
like. Our family decision usually comes up when we're asked, "Did you see so
and so on TV last night?" We've learned to say, "No, we didn't see it." That
way the conversation continues often without mention of the fact that we don't
have a TV in the home.

For us, this was a very personal decision and not something we push on
people. When asked, we just describe all the great benefits we've experienced.
Several have said they wished they could do the same, followed by a list of rea-
sons why it would be too difficult for them. Although none have gone to the

extreme of getting rid of their TVs, several have told us they were inspired to at least limit the viewing by their children.

Martha, Arvada, Colorado: *In 1996 we stopped watching regular television altogether with the exception of children's videos (mostly old Disney titles) and one or two PBS programs a year. The longer I'm away from it, the more shocked I am by the violence and immorality of both the show content and the advertisements those times I may catch a glimpse at a friend's home or in the mall.*

Ron & Michelle, Dallas, Texas: *We are happy to say that for the past three years we have not had a TV in our house. Simply, we feel that the images, commercialism, language, morality, spiritual message, temptation, waste of time, influence, hindrance to communication in our house, and materialism are not in line with our Christian beliefs.*

Like many other people, we recognize that there are some quality programs on TV. Unfortunately, we cannot trust the commercials to be acceptable and therefore have, under our personal convictions, removed the TV.

People are always referring to a TV program at work or while at dinner, and they usually forget that we do not have a TV. Our parents can't seem to understand why we don't have one. It's also intriguing to see how defensive people (especially Christians) become when the topic comes up that we do not have a TV. We always make it clear that it's a personal conviction. We do not think it is necessarily wrong for others to have a TV. Yet we often find that people start reciting their justification for having a TV—without us even asking them to justify it. For us, we're just better off without it, and we support you in your quest to limit TV in people's lives.

John and Jamie, Midlothian, Virginia: *My husband and I can testify to your belief that living without television has the power to revolutionize our relationships with our spouses, our children, our world, and with God. About four years ago my husband and I searched our hearts to determine things that might be hindering our walk with Christ. The television did cross our minds! Frankly, we couldn't find much that was helpful to us on television—physically, spiritually, or mentally.*

What's more, often when we'd sit down to watch just one show, we'd end up staring mindlessly at it until time for bed. But give up television? It seemed impossible. The weeks and months went by, and we continued to sense the Lord's urging to give up television. (Philippians 4:8 weighed heavy on our hearts.)

In May 1996 we finally sold our TV set and have lived without one for four years. People are often surprised, even amazed, when they discover we don't have a television. We just list for them the wonderful blessings being TV-free has brought into our lives. At the top of that list, we've discovered that the warfare in our minds has been reduced because so much of the world's influence was eliminated when the TV went out the door. We plan to encourage others to take your TV-turnoff challenge. The rewards truly are remarkable for those who do!

Michael and Kathy, Villa Park, Illinois: *Hi, Bob. I heard your interview a few weeks ago on WMBI in Chicago regarding your book on giving up TV. My husband and I disconnected cable in June of 1998 and never got around to getting an antenna, so we have been TV-less for thirteen months. About the only viewing we do comes from renting two or three movies a month. We were amazed by the way watching TV (especially advertising!) affected our attitudes and more subtly our values. We felt convicted that we should let it go, and we're doing just fine without it.*

Kimberly, Sharon Hill, Pennsylvania: *We gave away our televisions and VCRs in the summer of 1996. My son, who was ten at the time, appeared to be addicted to TV. It got to the point that he was becoming deceitful and untrustworthy in regard to television. TV became more of a hassle than it was worth. I decided it had to go—and it did.*

Funny, I noticed that my son became much more focused. His aggression decreased dramatically (no more Ninja Turtles or Power Rangers to imitate). He is still a reforming addict. This is evident whenever we go to visit people. He's drawn to their TV like a magnet.

Sure, I miss a few shows that I liked a lot, and I would enjoy watching videos on occasion. However, I will not allow TV back in my home. That may sound harsh, but I will not compromise my son and his character for a few hours of personal pleasure. I visit my family when I want to watch TV. (It's always on at my mom's and brothers' homes.)

I have no idea how I would get anything done if I had TV at home again. I have no spare time as it is! We listen to radio (music, drama, and teaching), tapes (Adventures in Odyssey from Focus on the Family is terrific!), and CDs, books on tape, etc. I find that this engages the imagination much more than the TV ever did.

Stephanie, Lyerly, Georgia: *I'm the mom of two preschoolers (ages four and two). We disconnected cable about four and a half years ago, although we kept PBS and the networks since my hubby had to have his football, and I had to have the one-eyed baby-sitter. Then in the summer of 1999 we built a house and moved where there's virtually no TV reception.*

So far I have been successful in not purchasing an antenna or signing up for a satellite service (we're in the middle of nowhere, so cable is not an option). I LOVE IT! My husband is accepting it. I've mentioned the benefits of no TV to several friends who find it hard to believe there are benefits. Trust me, I feel like I could write a book about not having a television.

THAT'S ALL, FOLKS

As I mentioned during the introduction to this book, it has been my *conviction* that anyone possessing the courage and the willpower to click off the TV for a brief season would experience life-changing results. Now it's my *prayer* that God has—and will—continue to revolutionize your relationships with each other and, most importantly, with Him.

What better treasure could there be?

I wish I had the room to reprint almost all of the journals I received from those who went TV-free for a month. You'd find these personal stories inspiring. While space doesn't permit that luxury, I have included one final journal.

I'd like to introduce you to Carl and Jennifer of Pottstown, Pennsylvania, a suburb of Philadelphia. This couple completed my TV-free challenge and has quite a story to tell. They're in their late twenties and early thirties and have a daughter, age "almost three," as well as a six-month-old bundle of joy. By her own admission, Jennifer was a "TV-aholic." She watched from four to seven hours a day. Jennifer told me, "I even had the whole TV schedule in my head!"

These folks decided to take the TV-free challenge during the early spring of 2000 in response to my being interviewed by Mark Daniels over Philadelphia's station WFIL. Following that interview Mark felt inspired to challenge his listeners to take the thirty-day TV-free challenge. More than a hundred listeners responded.

Several weeks after they had submitted their journal, I called Jennifer (who was primarily responsible for the journal entries) to secure her permission to reprint it. She was thrilled!

As we talked, Jennifer made this key observation: "Looking back, I see that month with no television as a gift. It enabled me to create a new habit. And while we occasionally watch television now, I find I don't have to fall back into the pattern of sitting for hours before the TV because I proved to myself I could live without it."

Thanks, Jennifer, for sharing your story with us.

THE JOURNAL OF CARL AND JENNIFER

DAY 1 ▪ *Today's the day—the first day of our Big TV Turnoff. It's snowing outside, my throat is scratchy, and the house is a wreck. We usually start the morning with* Dragon Tales *for my daughter Grace and a bit of* Later Today *for Mom. It's 8:17 A.M., and I must admit it seems like it's going to be a long day. But I'm claiming Philippians 4:13: "I can do everything through Christ who gives me strength."*

DAY 2 ▪ *I have to admit the first day wasn't too bad. It helped that the girls and I have previously had our own "no-TV" days. What's different is stringing the no-TV days together for a whole month. The most difficult time of the day seems to be after naptime and after dinner. For a diversion we played the piano, read books, and finally visited friends. They, like everyone else, thought we were crazy to go a month without TV. They also assured us that they could NEVER do it. We'll see. I occasionally have doubts as well!*

DAY 3 ▪ *Yesterday was rough! The day seemed to drag on and on. There were some highlights. Instead of watching TV, we listened to music, and my husband, Carl, played with Grace, and I played with the baby. The girls are definitely getting more attention since the TV has been off. Hopefully, the weather will allow us to get outside instead of sitting around trying to avoid turning on the television.*

DAY 4 ▪ *Yesterday was rough again. I broke down and watched 60 Minutes (my favorite show). My husband was home today, but nonetheless the time dragged on and on. I'm trying to find the Lord's way of escape from my temptation, and He has been faithful. Friends have called out of the blue scheduling enjoyable activities. And the phone has rung at just the right moment. "Lord, make me ever mindful of Your strength when I'm tempted."*

DAY 5 ▪ *Today wasn't so bad. A local Christian radio show called me asking me to share my experience on the air next Tuesday. We will be almost halfway through the thirty days, so I should have a good idea of how it is going. Actually, the call was very helpful. Knowing I'm going to be on the radio provides incentive and accountability. Praise God, He knows just what I need to stay on track!*

DAY 6 ▪ *This day was the best of times and the worst of times. We went out to a friend's house for most of the day, so the temptation was less. However, when we returned home, just the sheer exhaustion from the day enabled temptation to loom large. "Come on . . . sit down and relax," the TV seemed to beckon. Thankfully, having survived for five days, I've built up a momentum, so it appears at least for now we will overcome.*

DAY 7 ▪ *Wow—a whole week already! I had a friend come over today to help me clean, and later we exercised down in the basement, so the time passed quickly. She fully supports my TV turnoff. I explained that this time represents a "gift to God," much like a fast from food. She has tried unsuccessfully to talk her seven-year-old into doing their own turnoff.*

DAY 8 ▪ *I am definitely coming down with a cold. My human reasoning says it's because instead of relaxing with the television at night, I'm working around the house. I hope this isn't accurate. I find myself actually enjoying no TV! I do not want to go back to the way we were (four to seven hours of TV a day). My nearly three-year-old is not even asking about the television. She has adjusted better than I have! I thought she needed the TV for entertainment. But by day five, she was beginning to entertain herself. In fact, things I couldn't get her to do (like watercolors) she was asking for. The weather allowed a few walks and trips to the park, which she prefers to TV any day!*

DAY 9 ▪ *Talk about a long and dreary day! I'm still fighting a cold in earnest now. I did no housework. Instead I started and finished* Wuthering Heights. *Here is definitely an inspirational book. TV wasn't even 100 years away. The characters entertained themselves with walking, reading, dancing, singing, and, as in this book, falling in and out of love. I must admit these days of no TV are starting to feel like a long time.*

DAY 10 ▪ *Sorry to belabor the point, but I'm really feeling rough! The temptation to veg out in front of the TV has never been stronger. To counteract this, I telephoned a few friends. I made it to 7 P.M. Then, like last week, I gave into* 60 Minutes. *I know this is rationalizing, but it doesn't feel like TV. It's more like reading the front page of the newspaper. I must note, though, after having no television for ten days, the commercials seemed silly and intrusive.*

DAY 11 ▪ *It's confirmed. The doctor says I have bronchitis. Oh, well, maybe now with antibiotics I can be on the mend and start venturing out of the house again. I know it sounds crazy, but this illness really feels like a spiritual attack. Just when I was determined to focus on Christ for my friendship, my ability to go out is compromised, and I'm stuck at home, left to struggle with the temptation of television.*

DAY 12 ▪ *Today is the day for that radio interview. As I ponder what I may say, it occurs to me that turning off the television will mean different things to different people. For myself, a confessed TV-aholic, shutting off the tube was an absolute necessity. For others, like my husband, it was no big deal. But for the most of us, I do believe today's television is of little value. It constitutes a dangerous habit of amusement. Truly TV is a one-way conversation, mostly about the world's view of life. What's more, it demands that all of us just sit and "be quiet"!*

DAY 13 ▪ *Today was a really good day. I commented on the radio that I had "challenged" God to fill the vacuum left by TV, and He certainly is faithful. I don't believe I had a free moment to myself. From taking a walk to the park, to making fresh pasta, to a trip to McDonald's playland, I didn't even have the time to think about television. I'm discovering how refreshed I feel, not knowing all the trash—otherwise known as the "news"—about murders, lies, and smut going on in the world. Being TV-free has somehow caused me to savor the innocence found in my children even more.*

DAY 14 ▪ *Same old, same old . . . however, one observation. Without the TV as an option I'm sitting less and walking more, which is good, considering I still have about ten pounds from the second baby to lose. Instead of basking in the light of TV, it's housework—which is never quite done, so I always have something to do.*

DAY 15 ▪ *The halfway point! My husband left for Boston today, and the remote control is left unguarded. In a moment of madness, I turn on the television. Wait, there isn't that rush I used to get. There's repulsion. A stupid commercial comes on—the one where the car floats offstage and rides across mounds of hands. At the bottom of the screen it reads, "Always drive on roads, not on people." Yuck! How stupid can a commercial get? Quickly I shut it off. I'm slightly ashamed. Is this the trash I've been "keeping" myself from and yet still wanting? What does that say about me?*

DAY 16 ▪ *Well, I fell off the ol' TV wagon so to speak . . . no, no, not regular TV. With my hubby gone and the girls driving me bonkers, I resort to watching "The Riverdance" and Lawrence Welk. Wholesome stuff, I know. But TV nonetheless. It's survival mode now. Carl returns tomorrow. Praise God!*

DAY 17 ▪ *Funny how once the TV is on, it sure is hard to shut it off. Since I have a greater conviction not to do housework on Sunday than I do about not watching TV, I'm left idle. With church in the morning, followed by lunch and naptime, the day glides on smoothly. It's the evening that's tough. First, it's 60 Minutes—highly enjoyable, I might add. Then it's the "Three Irish Tenors" (a PBS pledge-week lure), which unfortunately works its magic on me. "It's not TV," I rationalize. "It's music." Starting tomorrow, I promise it's back to cold turkey no TV.*

DAY 18 ▪ *Twelve days to go. It's not that I want to go back to the way things were. On the contrary, I'm determined that we won't slip into old habits. With the strength of the Holy Spirit, I'll succeed. However, this is not to say I don't miss the occasional "Veggie Tale" for Gracie, and I want to watch* 60 Minutes *without guilt. They say the success of a good diet allows a bit of cheating. In other words, I won't miss being so legalistic about it.*

DAY 19 ▪ *My husband has been home, and it's been apparent that he sees no harm in popping in a video or two for Grace. I've unsuccessfully tried to convince him that a walk to the park or reading books is better than a video. This is on top of the fact that we, as a family, are on a TV fast. He reasons that since I don't let Grace watch television at all, what's the harm in a half-hour Christian video? I explain it's a matter of good versus excellent use of one's time.*

DAY 20 ▪ *Sent out a bunch of letters today. I really love writing. People have asked recently where I've found the time. It's amazing how much time is wasted in front of the ol' boob tube. I've decided when the thirty days are finished that not much will change. I really like how our life has changed for the better without the heavy use of television.*

DAY 21 ▪ *I've noticed that the television has had no pull for me lately. Oh, every now and then when the girls are both fussy, I'm tempted to turn it on. But other than that, it's covered with the tablecloth, and I don't even think about it. Strange—right before this fast, clicking it on and surfing the stations seemed the highlight of the day. Now, like an old love, I wonder "what did I ever see in it?"*

DAY 22 ▪ *It's my birthday! I can't think of a greater gift to give myself than that of time. What a precious commodity—time. You spend it only once. You can't earn interest on it. Everyone gets the same amount—twenty-four hours a day. I've really noticed how much I get done in the morning now that I'm not vegging in front of the boob tube. By the way, I've lost four pounds since shutting off the TV. Yeah!*

DAY 23 ▪ *Oh no, it's the beginning of a cold again, and it looks like the whole family is in for it this time. But the weather is warm, so it's time for the park and getting out of the house anyway.*

DAY 24 ▪ *We are all home with harmless but annoying colds. We just sit around and sniffle. After a while Grace plays outside with Dad while he does yard work. I stay inside and play with the baby.*

DAY 25 ▪ *As you can probably tell, I haven't felt much like writing in my journal. I've been busy sending out my monthly letter to friends and family who live far away. I admit, like a weed, some TV has snuck back into our life. Gotta work on it.*

DAY 26 ▪ *Been really tempted to just give up, but I haven't. I know it sounds silly being this close to the end. But with the kids being miserable and me feeling even worse, vegging out with the TV seems like a viable option—not to mention, the weather's cold these days.*

DAY 27 ▪ *Hubby brought home an A&E video classic on Charles Dickens. After an exhausting and frustrating day of laundry, potty training, and separation anxiety from the TV, frankly the video was a welcome treat. One observation about videos: Aside from the few commercials at the beginning, which you can fast-forward through, the video program comes without commercials. Commercials are even worse than watching the shows in terms of being time-wasters. After being away from them for thirty days, I don't think I can tolerate going back to them.*

DAY 28 ▪ *Gave into the temptation to turn on the television. I turned on The View—a trashy show I didn't even watch back when I was watching TV. After just two minutes of discussing sex (hmm, what a surprise!), I shut it off in disgust. It just reinforced the obvious. After thirty days of life with no TV, I've concluded there is no TV worth watching.*

DAY 29 ▪ *With the weather grim outside and attitudes bored inside, we give in to a few Christian videos. I must admit animated stories from the Bible really bring the Bible alive for Grace.*

DAY 30 ▪ *I didn't think we'd make it . . . and toward the end we saw a few more videos than allowed, but we certainly fasted from the TV for a good, long while. Most important, we broke our addiction to TV in our home! And I'm thrilled by how it benefited both our spiritual life and marriage. I know for sure it has helped my prayer life. I felt as if God was honoring our desire to cut back on TV, and as a result my prayer life is much more dynamic. Thank you for extending this chance to be a part of something so life changing.*

For twenty years I've studied the impact of pop culture on the family and authored several books on Christian discernment. As I prepared to write this book, I asked people of all ages to consider exploring the question: "What would life be like without TV for thirty days?"

To that end, I asked whether they could imagine saying, "See ya later, Leno"? Would life still be rosy without Rosie? You might enjoy considering your responses to these questions. In fact, I'd encourage you to copy and reprint this survey for use in your church, small group, or school. If you use it in a small-group setting, I'd appreciate it if you'd cite this book as the source for the survey.

Have fun tackling these questions!

THE FIVE-MINUTE TV SURVEY

Name _____

Address _____

City/State/Zip _____

1. Family profile *(check one)*: ☐ Married
   ☐ Single, never married
   ☐ Single parent

2. How has television had a POSITIVE effect on your Christian growth?

3. How has television had a NEGATIVE effect on your Christian growth?

4. Were you ever offended by the content of a television show? If so, please provide an example. Did you do anything about it?

5. How frequently is the TV on:

during breakfast? ☐ Most of the time
☐ Occasionally
☐ Never

during dinner? ☐ Most of the time
☐ Occasionally
☐ Never

6. Would your family find it relatively easy, somewhat difficult, or almost impossible to go thirty days without TV? *(circle one)*

7. What might prevent your family from trying a thirty-day TV fast?

8. Was there a time when your family had to go without TV for a
   day or more due to a power failure, broken TV, or activity such
   as camping? If so, describe what life was like without TV.

9. If you don't own a TV, why not? How has the TV-free life
   affected your home?

OTHER RESOURCES FROM BOB DEMOSS

Books

21 Days to Better Family Entertainment (Zondervan), 1998
Learn to Discern (Zondervan), 1997
Sex & the Single Person (Zondervan), 1995

Seminars

"A Generation at Risk"—A multimedia examination of music, media, and pop culture, designed for college and adult audiences.

"Hope for the Single Heart"—A seminar presentation designed to help singles deal with issues of intimacy and sexuality.

For booking information, write:

Bob DeMoss
P.O. Box 20
Franklin, TN 37065

NOTES

PART ONE

1. Groucho Marx, quoted in *Columbia Dictionary of Quotations* (New York: Columbia University Press, 1993), 899.
2. "TV Forever Changes Alaskan Tribe," Associated Press, May 22, 1999.
3. Ibid.
4. Ibid.
5. John Marks Templeton, *Discovering the Laws of Life* (Radnor, Penn.: Templeton Foundation Press, 1995), 236.
6. Ibid.
7. Ibid.
8. *Rolling Stone,* May 14, 1998, 68.
9. *Citizen Issues Alert,* April 8, 1998.
10. Woody Allen, in the film *Annie Hall,* 1977.
11. Gary Levin, *USA Today,* September 23, 1999.
12. "And now . . . smut-see TV," *U.S. News & World Report,* September 27, 1999, 15.
13. Ibid.
14. "What is causing our moral decline?" *USA Today,* August 2, 1999.
15. John Grisham, taken from an AOL on-line chat session.
16. "Broken VCRs Played a Part in Capitals Surge," *Associated Press,* February 2, 2000.
17. Ibid.
18. Susan R. Johnson, M.D., "Strangers in Our Homes: TV and Our Children's Minds," http://sooth.com/a/johnson.html, 1999, page 7.
19. Rosalie Maggio, *Quotations by Women* (Boston, Mass.: Beacon Press, 1996), 685.
20. Robert Andrews, *The Columbia Dictionary of Quotations* (New York: Columbia University Press, 1993), 762.
21. Maggio, *Quotations by Women,* 685.
22. Michael Moncur, *Michael Moncur's Collection of Quotations* (from an on-line Internet document).

PART TWO

1. Landers, *Wake Up and Smell the Coffee!* (New York: Villard Books, 1996), 356.
2. "New Study Finds Best Thing for Keeping Kids Off Drugs," *Fatherhood Today,* Fall 1999, 5.
3. Ibid.
4. Ann Landers, "Save Your Marriage, Buy Another TV," *The Tennessean,* February 16, 2000, 2D.
5. David Louis, *2201 Fascinating Facts* (New York: Wings Books, 1983), 289.